ASST. PROF. DR. RAHMI ORUC GUVENC
THE ETERNAL SHEIKH

Aziz Serhat Kural

ACKNOWLEDGEMENT

I owe a debt of gratitude to Yasar Guvenc, Andrea Azize Guvenc, Kanikey Guvenc-Akcay and Emre Basaran for their material and spiritual support during the preparation of this book.

CONTENT

HOW I MET ORUÇ GÜVENÇ

Believe me, it never occurred to me that I would write this book. In fact, when the thought of writing a book about Oruc Guvenc first came to my mind, I asked my friend Emre Basaran, a close associate of Mr. Oruc Guvenc in his musical and spiritual endeavors, whether he might carry out such a project. In reply, he told me that it would be more appropriate if I took care of the matter.

That is why I would like to start with how I met Oruc Bey. It was either 1979 or 80 and I was playing in a chess tournament. A long time has passed since then, so I don't remember exactly which tournament it was, but I think it was the Musa Tebi Memorial Tournament, where I finished among the top three and received a small monetary prize. At this tournament, I was playing against Ali Ipek, who later went on to win the FIDE Master title[1].

Ali made a sidelong attack from his King's side, deftly capturing my Castle with his Bishop. At that point, I believe he thought he had won the game. But after he captured my Castle, I was able to retrieve the pieces I had lost and improve my position with a particular pawn move. Ali, surprised by my pawn maneuver, had to think long and hard as to what to play next. In the end the game was adjourned. In the late 70s and early 80s there was no internet or personal computers, and smart phones were not yet available. In those days, if a chess game took too long, it was adjourned and continued at a later date determined by the referee. However nowadays, since it is possible to analyze a game with computers, with a few modifications the 'Guillotine' or 'Sudden Death' system is applied, whereby a player who exceeds the time limit immediately loses the game. Anyway, the game was adjourned, and I was one pawn up. I went home and realized that, despite being a pawn up, I was losing in a problematic fashion. However, I was aware that my opponent might not be able to see this because any normal analysis would have indicated that I was winning.

With many thoughts in my mind, I arrived at the chess center on the day the game was to resume. Ali had also come. We talked and decided between us that the game should end in a draw, without further play. Afterwards, when Ali commented that I could have won, I showed him the

---

1   A Master Title of the International Chess Federation (FIDE)

intricate moves he could have made to win. He was amazed and sat lost in thought for a while. He then said he wanted to take me somewhere. On the way, he told me that he wanted to introduce me to a Sufi Master.

At that time, I was totally unaware that the ensuing interaction would totally and profoundly affect the rest of my life. On the bus, Ali explained that this person was a great Master and an expert in Sufism, Music and Turkhood. Finally, we arrived at Oruc Bey[2]'s 3-storied timber villa in Kadirga. If I remember correctly, Ali had a key. We went inside. There was a wooden staircase to the left of the entrance that went up to the first and second floors. The first floor was used most of the time and the rooms on the upper floors were used for specific purposes. We stayed on the first floor where musical instruments were hanging from all the walls, some of which I had never seen before. Some instruments that I found most

During a conversation with Oruc Bey

intriguing lay on the floor looking like mere boxes covered with lots of taut strings, which I later learned to be Indian instruments. It was there, on the first floor, that I first met Oruc Bey.

I shall never forget how, on reaching the first floor, we entered the room on the right where I saw him playing 'El Condor Pasa' to me on a Shakuhachi (a Japanese flute made from bamboo). I immediately warmed to him and that has continued to increase to this day. It would be no exaggeration to say that our Sheikh-disciple relation started at that very moment.

That evening, or in the following days I don't quite remember, Ali explained why he took me to meet Oruc Bey. He said that, after the match I mentioned earlier, he had experienced a chronic headache for which aspirin and similar medication did little to help, so he had gone to consult Oruc Bey. According to Ali, Oruc Bey had explained the reason for the headache as follows: "A knot formed in your mind when you thought you had lost your Bishop while playing chess against a long-haired boy with a light beard. This is the reason for your headache. Bring that boy to me,

<hr>

2 'Bey' is used as 'Mr.' or 'Sire/Sir' in Turkish. However, note that it follows the first name instead of the surname, as in the West.

whenever it is convenient for you."

Yes, that is how I met Oruc Bey, but this book is about Oruc Bey. If this book attracts attention and if there is demand, I would very much like to write about my apprenticeship with him. But my aim in this book is to outline the life and works of Rahmi Oruc Guvenc and provide insight into his teachings. I have no wish to crowd the book with details like dates, places and names.

ETHNIC ORIGINS AND CHILDHOOD

"One side of my family lineage is from Kazan Turks, the other side from Kyrgyz Turks. We would listen to music performed by our family from early childhood and this music (pentatonic music) became essential for me."[3]

Before moving on to the musical aspect of Oruc Bey's life, I want to tell you a little about his ethnic origins. As the above quotation says, Oruc Bey had Central Asian ancestry. His father, Ahmet Kamil Guvenc, was born into a family that migrated from Tatarstan to Tavsanli/Kutahya during the 93 war[4]. A short biography of Ahmet Kamil Guvenc, written by Yasar Guvenc, elder brother of Oruc Bey and Ahmet Kamil Guvenc's other son, provides some important details:

Kamil and Urkiye Guvenc

"Ahmet Kamil Guvenc was born into a family that had migrated during the 93 war and settled in Hamitabat Village close to Tavsanli[5]. His father Abdussukur was martyred in the war of the Dardanelles, which was why his they came with their mother to Tavsanli. As a young man, Ahmet Kamil repaired watches and gramophones and he sold bicycles, gramophones and watches. In 1948, he brought out the 'Tavsanli Post' (Tavsanli Postasi) newspaper, which was published daily and weekly for over 40 years.

"In 1952, Ahmet Kamil Guvenc established the first printing house in Tavsanli and trained many typographers. He put a lot of

---

3   TRT Vision magazine, August 2017, p.12
4   Ottoman-Russian War of 1877-1878, which was known as the 93 War because it corresponded
    to the date of 1293 in the Rumi Calendar
5   A township in the province of Kutahya in Western Anatolia.

effort into developing Tavsanli and started a campaign for the re-forestation and reorganization of an area called Mulayim Dede[6]. He published 2 books, 'Garden of Thorns 1'and 'Garden of Thorns 2' (Dikenli Bahce-1 and Dikenli Bahce-2), which depicted the residents and workers of Tavsanli. Later, he published a book called Old-New Riddles and Turkish Poems[7]. In 1978, he built and moved into a house on the road to Dedeler Village, which was later named Kamil Guvenc Avenue, and he would walk to Tavsanli and back every day to keep fit. He was awarded certificates of gratitude by the Kutahya Journalists Association and the Tavsanli Municipality. In 1990, he went with his sons Oruc and Yasar to live in Istanbul, where he died on 24th Januar 2001, exactly 2 years after his wife Urkiye Guvenc, next to whom he was buried in Karacaahmet Cemeter."

I encountered Kamil Bey personally a few times. One time was at a photography exhibition by Oruc Bey's wife's at Hikmet Barutcugil's Ebru Centre (Ebristan[8]) in Uskudar[9]. I had a conversation with Kamil Bey over tea and snacks and he told me stories of his family's migration from Central Asia. On another occasion, a television channel interviewed Kamil Bey and his wife Lady Urkiye at Oruc Bey's place in Cerrahpasa (the Ethnomusicology Center) about their experiences during the War of Independence.

Kamil Bey displayed a humorous side to his character with his intolerance towards Oruc Bey's diet[10]. One time when he came to Cerrahpasa, I accompanied him to the bus stop for his return journey and noticed that he was taking home a nylon bag of Knorr tomato soups, which made me smile inwardly. I heard from others that he would sometimes visit fish restaurants and feast on fish until late in the evening. I should mention here that fish and tomatoes are foods that Oruc Bey never ate.

Rahmi Oruc Guvenc, the second son of Ahmet Kamil and Urkiye Guvenc, was born in 1948. Urkiye Guvenc was a housewife and Oruc Bey was the middle of three siblings. Oruc Guvenc completed his primary and intermediate level education in Tavsanli, and his high school education in Kutahya.

---

6 An area in Tavsanli
7 These are poems formed of stanzas (M'ani) - a Turkish tradition
8 A marbling center
9 A neighbourhood in the Asian side of Istanbul
10 I will give detailed information later about the strict diet followed by Oruc Bey .

(From Left to Right) Oruc Bey, Kamil and Urkiye Guvenc, his father and mother) Nejat Guvenc (his younger brother) and Yasar Guvenc (his elder brother)

Returning to the quotation at the start of this section, Oruc Bey frequently talked about how they grew up listening to pentatonic music and melodies. According to his beliefs and research, children should listen to nothing but pentatonic music until the ages of 9 or 10. As we will see in the following section 'Oruc Bey and Music', pentatonic music is the basic tonality of Turkish music. Before the transition to 'makam[11]' music, there was pentatonic music, a structure which is still being preserved especially in Central Asia. Pentatonic music is used in the therapy system applied at the Nordoff Robbins Centre in London, where it is held to induce feelings of self-confidence and self-determination.

---

11 In pentatonic music there are 5 tones whereas in 'makam' music there are 7 tones

ORUC BEY'S ACQUAINTANCE WITH SUFISM

If I am not mistaken, we were at Gokcedere for a Sema[12] lasting 99 days and nights. I was asked to help with the English sections of a literary work that was later to be sold, in spiral binding and trilingual format, under the title "Dr. Rahmi Oruc Guvenc, Compositions and Lyrics". I translated 30-35 poems into English for that work. In one of the poems, Oruc Bey poetized and encapsulated his entrancement by a blond, green eyed lady, who was one of his pupils. While Oruc Bey was sitting in his place at the Dergah[13], I referred to this lady with a few rather humorous words. My intention was to tease him a bit and create a jolly atmosphere – that is how intimate we were with Oruc Bey. Realizing that my intentions were quite innocent, he added that it was in the same period of his life that he had become "acquainted with Sufism (Tasavvuf)".

To be acquainted with Sufism, to become informed about these subjects, is a gift that isn't granted to just anyone. Years ago, in either 1976-77 or 78, when the former head of the Turkish Metapsychic Investigations and Scientific Research Association Ergun Arikdal was still alive, I attended a few of his significant conferences there. At that time, there was no social media, no videos and no smart phones. You could only learn new things through books, magazines or by gathering together somewhere. At one of these conferences, Ergun Arikdal iterated that many people are born, grow up and die without ever knowing or even encountering Sufism, or other such subjects that deal matters beyond the scope of physical cognition. That is why to be acquainted with Sufism means to be bestowed with a gift and it is a significant milestone in one's life. I have reached this conclusion from my own experiences.

Oruc Bey had already become acquainted with spiritualism through a magazine called 'Soul and Matter'[14] magazine to which their father Kamil Guvenc subscribed. They began their first attempts at hypnosis in Tavsanli with a photographer called Ilhan Birlik. They would either gather in Ilhan Birlik's photography studio or, if convenient, at his father's print-

---

12 A gathering of Sufis to perform the whirling rituals of the Mevlevite and other orders. I will give detailed explanation on this in the following chapters.

13 Dergah is a sacred place where dervishes of a certain order gather or live.

14 A monthly magazine that was published by the above-mentioned Meta Psychic Investigations and Scientific Research Association.

ing house, and carried out hypnotism, spiritism and regression[15] practices. These practices went on for approximately 3 years. Oruc Bey's elder brother Yasar Guvenc, from whom we have acquired these details, was also attending these practices. One day, Yasar Bey took a largish walnut table, that needed at least 4 or 5 people to lift, to the practice of a dentist called Ferhan Bey. The session operator Ferhan Bey, the mediums and other attendees took their seats around the table. The session started. An entity arrived, lifting the walnut table a little and then letting it bang on the floor. The legs of the walnut table were suddenly rising 2 hand spans above the floor and then banging back down to the floor. This was how the entity was making its presence known and answering questions. One strike meant 'yes', and two strikes meant 'no'. When writing words, one strike was taken to be an 'A', two strikes a 'B', three a 'C', and so on. When asked who he was, the entity gave the name of 'Neyzen Tevfik'[16]. After a period of questions and answers, a message came from the entity, saying ' Compose'. When asked 'Who should compose?', they received the name of Neyzen Hayri Bey, who was present at the seance. When asked 'What should he compose?', three loud knocks came from behind a portrait of Neyzen Tevfik that hung on the wall. The picture, which depicted him in a trance with a stanza that he had purportedly received while in the trance, shook violently. I give the stanza below:

Don't judge by looking at the image
That image is contemplating God
So what if you always see Neyzen drunk
He is constructing the Kaaba in the tavern

Oruc Bey's meeting with his first Master took place around the age of 18. He was informed of the matter at a spiritism session similar to the one I described above and actually met his first Master Fazyl Bey (His Holiness Fazyl Guvey) a few days later. Fazyl Bey was an Imam[17] who had undergone special training and worked as an Imam in various neighborhoods, including Dedeler Village. Fazyl Bey provided spiritual guidance to Oruc Bey and Yasar Agabey[18] with lengthy narrations. We learn from Yasar Aga-

15 The practice of regression to past lives under hypnosis.
16 A great Sufi and a virtuose Ney player known for his satirical poems targeting politicians and the general state of affairs. A Ney is a reed flute, usually associated with the Mevlevite order or Sufism in general. Neyzen means 'Ney player'.
17 Imam is a religious minister who leads the prayers and who also has other duties.
18 Agabey literaly means elder brother and is used very commonly for show respect to people who you are close to and are older in terms of age.

bey that, after a certain point in their spiritual education, they stopped asking questions and simply listened. Oruc Bey and Yasar Agabey received spiritual instruction from Fazyl Bey for approximately 3 years. Fazyl Bey, was a disciple of His Holiness Seyyid Ahmed Husamettin, a grandson of our Prophet (mPbuH) 40 times removed. His Holiness Seyyid Ahmed Husamettin came to Istanbul with his father from Dagestan during the reign of Sultan Abdulmejid (1839-1861).

You might be asking why from Dagestan and not from some Arab country. It is a very long story. I would like to recommend reading works on the life of His Holiness Seyyid Ahmed Husamettin, but I don't want to cut corners here without giving some important information. First let's answer the question why Dagestan[19]?

It was the era when Arabs were conquering Central Asia. The Transoxiana region (the area between the Amu Darya and Syr Darya rivers which today covers parts of Turkmenia, Uzbekistan and Kazakstan) was being conquered by Arabian armies. But some cruel Arabian rulers were badly mistreating descendants of our Prophet (mPbuH), who were being imprisoned, ostracized and even killed. As a result, some groups of these descendants of the Prophet (mP-buH) (ehlu'l-beyt) managed to join the Conquest Caravans without being perceived and migrated to Transoxiana, where they changed into Turkic clothing, referred to their villages with Turkic names and mixed with the

His Holiness Seyyid Sheikh Ahmed Husammettin

___

19 A former Soviet Republic in the Caucasus populated mainly by Tatars (a Turkic tribe) which
   now is a part of the Russian federation.

local people in order to erase any trace of who they were. This plan was successful and apparently was also unnoticed. These people were the ancestors of His Holiness Seyyid Ahmed Husamettin.

Here I want to go into the science of genetics a little. As you know, people who are descendants of His Holiness Hasan , Grandson of our Prophet (mPbuH), are called Sharifs and descendants of His Holiness Huseyin, His other grandson, are called Seyyids. During the development of modern genetics, the family tree of Seyyids has been investigated. The Y-DNA haplogroup can determine a paternal ancestor who lived ten thousand or so years ago. The Y-DNA haplogroups are formed through thousands of years of mutations of the Y-chromosome that is transferred from father to son. Haplogroups are identified with letters. The J1e haplogroup and some of its subclades belong to the Seyyids[20]. The J1 haplogroup is the main haplogroup in the Middle East and - yes you are not mistaken - it is also very common in Dagestan. Genetic research is verifying the journey taken by the ancestors of His Holiness Seyyid Ahmed Husamettin. In Dagestan, where Tatars[21] comprise a very large portion of the population, the J1 haplogroup has been very clearly identified as over 90% [22] in some clans.

The family tree of His Holiness Sheikh Husamettin is given below:

The family tree of Seyyids, who form the genealogy of our Prophet and are known as Ehl-i Beyt (the Household of the Prophet (mPbuH)), is depicted below with birth and death dates up to His Holiness Seyyid Ahmed Husammetin, 40th grandson of our Prophet (mPbuH):

---

20 DNA is able to Illuminate Islam's Lineage -https://www.thenational.ae/uae/dna-could-illuminate-islam-s-lineage-1.504829
21 A Turkic tribe
22 https://www.haplogroups.org/haplogroup-j1-y-dna-m267

Her Holiness Fatima (mPbuH)	(608-632)
His Holiness Huseyin (mPbuH)	(625-682)
Seyyid Ali Zeynelâbidin	(658-712)
Seyyid Muhammed Bakyr	(676-732)
Seyyid Jafer Sadyk 1	(699-765)
Seyyid Mûsâ Kâzym 1	(745-799)
Seyyid Ali Ryza	(760-S IS)
Seyyid Muhammed Cevad	(SI0-S35)
Seyyid Ebû afer Ali Hâdi	(829-867)
Seyyid Jafer Mahdi	(849-933)
Seyyid Ebulkasym Muhammed	(867-940)
Seyyid Abdulhâlyk 1	(883-965)
Seyyid Abdullah El Katim	(952-1004)
Seyyid Muhammed Ebû Tayyib	(975-1018)
Seyyid Abdulhâlyk 2	(1010-1084)
Seyyid Ali Zeynelâbidin	(1033-1075)
Seyyid Ebunnecâ Hasan	(1055-1116)
Seyyid Ebû Abdullah Mûsâddyk	(1095-1153)
Seyyid Kureysh Bin Muhammed	(1141-1209)
Seyyid Ebulmecd Abdullah	(1182-1249)
Seyyid Ebû Tahir Ibrahim	(1235-1277)
Seyyid Ebul Abbas Abdullah	(1257-1330)
Seyyid Isâ Ahrâr	(1285-1348)
Seyyid Ebuuhâshim Suleyman	(1307-1370)
Seyyid Ebû Ali Ahmed Bagdadî	(1354-1409)
Seyyid Ebul Avn Mustafa Ahrâr	(1369-1443)

Seyyid Ismail	(1398-1452)
Seyyid Ibrahim	(1423-1501)
Seyyid Mûsâ Kâzym 2	(1442-1502)
Seyyid Muhammed Zâhid	(1463-1538)
Seyyid Jafer Zeki 2	(1490-1535)
Seyyid Dâvud	(1519-1606)
Seyyid Ebû Hamza	(1558-1597)
Seyyid Kasym	(1589-1643)
Seyyid Ebû Hâmid Hasan	(1611-1688)
Seyyid Ali Haidar	
Seyyid Muhammed Mushtak	(1694-1775)
Seyyid Sefer	(1754-1824)
Seyyid Said Rukâlî	(1788-1871)
Seyyid Ahmed Husameddin	(1848-1925)
Seyyid Mehmed Ismetullah OZTURK	(1882-1952)
Seyyid Mûsâ Kâzym OZTURK	(1913 until 25 May 1996)

Returning to our story, His Holiness Fazyl Bey was called up for his military service and sent to join a unit in Balıkesir along with hundreds of other soldiers. The moment he got off the train, someone came up to him and asked, "Are you Fazyl?". When he answered "Yes", this person said, "Let's go!". Because Fazyl Bey was a dervish, he followed this person without asking any questions. They went together to His Holiness Seyyid Ahmed Husameddin, from whom Fazyl Bey received spiritual guidance throughout his military service.

One day, under the direction of His Holiness Seyyid Ahmed Husameddin and under the watch of his cousin Hafız Agabey (who was also in charge), His Holiness Fazyl Bey went up a few steps in the house where they were and entered a chamber in order to carry out a term of seclusion

(Halvet)[23]. On entering the chamber, he realized he was in fact on board a spaceship. He travelled and received guidance on this spaceship for 2000 years. When he returned, he found that no more than 3 days or a week had passed. His accounts of these journeys were very interesting. According to his narrations, there was life on the planet Mars. He also made references to some moon stones and, most interestingly, he stated that on one of the planets they reached, ants had established a very advanced civilization.

One day during the Eid al-Adha (The Sacrifice Festival), he said "What a shame that we kill and eat these animals", to which his Sheikh answered: "Their meat ascends in our (human) bodies."

On another occasion when His Holiness Fazyl Bey and his Sheikh were taking a stroll, they saw two olive kernels thrown by the side of the road. His Sheikh cleaned them with his hands and ate them, saying: "These kernels wait 2 thousand years to be able to pass through a human throat."

After Yasar Guvenc graduated from his school, he went to Konya on an errand and received news of Fazyl Bey's death.

When Oruc Bey came to Istanbul for his university education in 1960, he became acquainted with Turgut Baba[24] (Turgut Soylemezoglu) through Halil Konuralp. Turgut Baba claimed to be the last apprentice of Ahmed Jelaleddin Dede, who happened to be the last Mentor of the Galata Mevlevihane[25] in Istanbul. Oruc Bey had the opportunity of receiving guidance on Sufism (Tasavvuf) from Turgut Baba, with whom he stayed for a year or two. When Turgut Baba stopped teaching Oruc Bey, it left him feeling suspended in a void and of his own accord he embarked on fifty or sixty days of seclusion (Halvet). During this period of Halvet, he had a series of dreams and became acquainted with Ziya Efendi (Ziyaeddin Kudur), also known as Ayar Baba, in whose house he spent five or six months living in a cell that was allocated to him. His Holiness Ziyâ Efendi was a Mentor for the Sâdî Order and had also been granted permission to teach the beliefs and customs of the Kadirî, Ushshakî, Mevlevî, Bektashî and Rufaî orders[26]. After a while, Ziyâ Efendi granted Oruc Bey permission to teach the paths of these orders and also presented him with an ijazet (written ratification) to teach the path of the Sâdî order. The last section of this icazet contains the following story by His Holines Sadeddin Cibavi,

---

23 An Islamic practice of seclusion, like that of Tibetan hermits.
24 Baba and Dede are titles of mystical Masters.
25 A place where followers of the Mevlevite Order gather, live or perform religious practices.
26 Orders or Tarikats are dervish groups where a certain path is followed to reach enlightenment

written in slightly different words and in Ottoman script.

"It was rumoured that Saadeddin Cibavi, who had settled in the village of Cebâ between Havran and Damascus, had become involved in local banditry. His father Sheikh[27] Yunus esh-Sheybanî, who became very troubled on hearing that his son was even chief of these bandits, went into Halvet and prayed for his son's redemption. These prayers were answered and Sadeddin gave up his sinful activities, repented and embarked on the path of his father's order.

According to sources, one night Sadeddin dreamt that eleven men on white horses appeared before him and his friends. One of these horsemen recited the following Ayet (Qoranic verse): "Has not the time come for the believers to chant the name of Allah and feel a deep shudder due to the Qoran that has been revealed through Him?" (Hadid 57, 16). Whereupon Sadeddin and his friends fainted and fell from their horses. Later, when they regained consciousness, one of the horsemen said: "Sadeddin! I am your Prophet Muhammed (mPbuH) and these are my ten companions", whereupon he anointed Sadeddin's chest and asked him to repent, suggesting that he should chant to God

Sheikh Ezel Oruc Bey sitting on the Sheikh's Hide (Post) with His Sheikh Cloak, written ratification (ijazet), he mace of Arslan Bey and other depictive artifacts.

(zikir). He put a mantle around Sadeddin's shoulders and brought out three dates sent by His Holiness Ali over which he had exhaled, and gave these to Sadeddin to eat, saying, "Oh Sadeddin! Take these.

---

27 Sheikh here means a spiritual Master of an order – in this case the Sheybani order.

They are for you and all your descendants until doomsday comes."

This event depicts the innate inheritance of the order by Sadeddin Cibavi directly from Our Prophet (mPbuH). The details of this event were later to become elements that determined the character, modus and practices of the Sadiyye Order.

After this event, Sadeddin went to Mecca where he started to traverse the path of the Order and finished his education on Sufism at the side of his father Yunus esh-Sheybanî, founder of the Sheybaniyye branch of the Medyeniyye order. After receiving the mantle of the Order from his father, he returned to Ceba, where he constructed a mosque and a hermitage, and set about his duties for the Order.[28]

Oruc Bey was the Sheikh of these six[29] orders and known as 'Sheikh Ezel' (The Eternal Sheikh).

---

28 Http://www.rifai.org/sufism/turkce/tarikatler/sadiyye/ikinci-dogumu, last access: 15-09-2018
29 Kadirî, Ushshakî, Mevlevî, Bektashî, Sâdî and Rufaî orders.

ORUC BEY'S PRAYER[30]

Euzubillâhimineshsheytânirrajim
Bismillâh-irrahmân-irrahim.
Elhamdu lilâhi rabbil'âlemiyn.
Errahman-irrahiym.
Mâliki yevmiddin.
İyyâke na'budu ve iyyâke neste'iyn.
İhdina-siratal-mustekiym
Sirâtalleziyne en'amte 'aleyhim gayrilmagdubi 'aleyhim veladdâliyn.
(Âmin)

Innallâhe ve melâiketehi yusallune alen nebiyyi yâ eyyuhellezine amenu sallu aleyhi ve sellimu teslimâ. (Âmin)

Allâhumme salli ve sellim ve bârik âlâ seyyidinâ Muhammedin ve âlâ, âlihi ve eshâbihi ejmain.

Subhane rabbike rabbil izzeti ammâ yasifune ve selamun alel murselin velhâmdulillâhi rabbil âlemin.

Esselatu vesselam aleyke yâ Resulullah
Esselatu vesselam aleyke yâ habîballah
Esselatu vesselam aleyke yâ halilallah
Esselatu vesselam aleyke yâ nebiyyallah
Esselatu vesselam aleyke yâ safiyallah
Esselatu vesselam aleyke yâ hayre halkillah
Esselatu vesselam aleyke yâ nure arshillah
Esselatu vesselam aleyke yâ emine vahyillah
Esselatu vesselam aleyke yâ men zeyyenehullah
Esselatu vesselam aleyke yâ men sherrefehullah
Esselatu vesselam aleyke yâ men kerremehullah
Esselatu vesselam aleyke yâ men azzemehullah
Esselatu vesselam aleyke yâ men alleme hullah
Esselatu vesselam aleyke yâ seyyidel murselin
Esselatu vesselam aleyke yâ imâmel muttakin

---

30 Oruc Bey was given the prayer of the Kadiri Order known as the Evrad-i Sherife-i Kadiriyye. These prayers are chanted regularly at certain times.

Esselatu vesselam aleyke yâ hâtemen nebiyyin
Esselatu vesselam aleyke yâ rahmetellil âlemin
Esselatu vesselam aleyke yâ shefiul muznibin
Esselatu vesselam aleyke yâ rasule rabbilâlemin

Salavatullâhi ve melâiketihi ve enbiyâihi ve Resulihi ve hameleti
arshihi ve jemii halkihi âlâ seyyidinâ Muhammedin ve âlâ, âlihi ve
eshâbihi ejmain.

(Allâhumme salli âlâ seyyidinâ Muhammedin abdike ve Nebiike ve
Resuliken nebiyyil ummiyyi ve âlâ âlihi ve sahbihi ve sellim) x 3

(Allâhumme salli âlâ seyyidina Muhammedin innebiyyil melihi
sahibil makamil âlâ vellisanil fasih) x 3

Allâhummej'al efdâle salavâtike ebedâ ve enmâ berekâtike sermedâ
ve ez kâ tahiyyatike fadlan ve adedâ âlâ eshrefil halâikil insâniyye ve
mejmâil hakâikil imâniyye ve turit tejelliyâtil ihsaniyye be mehbitil
esrârir rahmâniyye ve arusil memleketir rabbâniyye ve vasitati ikdin
nebiyyin ve mukaddimi jeyshil murselin. Ve kâidi rekbil enbiyâil
mukerremin ve efdalil halki ejmain hâmili livâil izzil âlâ. Ve mâliki
ezimmetil mejdil esnâ shâhidi esrâril ezel. Ve mushâhidi envaris
sevâbikil uvvel. Ve terjemâni lisânil kidem, ve membail ilmi vel
hilmi vel hikem, mazhâri sirril judil juziyyi vel kulli ve insâni aynil
vujudil ulviyyi vesuffli.

Ruhi jesedil kevneyn x 3

Ve ayni hayatid dâreyni el mutahakkiku bi a'lâ rutebil ubudiyye vel
mutahalliku bi ahlâkil makâmâtil istifâiyye.

(Selam) El halilil âzam vel habibil ekrem seyyidinâ Muhammedin
Ibn-i Abdillah Ibn-i Abdil Mutallip ve âlâ Sâiril enbiyâil murselin
ve âlâ melâiketikel mukarrabin.

Ve âlâ ibadillâhis sâlihin, min ehlissemâvâti vel ehlil erdin ve gafele
an zikrikel gâfulune, ve sellim ve radiyallâhu ta'alâ an eshâbi Resulil-
lahi ejmain.

ORUC BEY'S DIET

"A body without a diet is like a fruitless tree; A human without shame is like a meal without salt; a body without conation is like an ownerless slave" - His Holiness Shams-i Tabrizî

I believe it was 1994 when I took part in a Sufi Tour[31] with Oruc Bey and the rest of the TUMATA ensemble. After stopping by in several cities, we arrived in Konya. For accommodation and lodging purposes Shams-i Tabrizî Hotel had been chosen. If I am not mistaken, the mausoleum of His Holiness Shams-i Tabrizî was right opposite the Hotel. While visiting there, I bought two books on Sufism from a chapman. The two maxims of His Holiness Shams that I learned from these books guided me for long periods of time. The first maxim was, "Mystical Science (Ilm-i Ledûn) consists of three things: A tongue that chants, a heart that is grateful, and a body that is patient.". The other maxim was, "A body without a diet is like a fruitless tree; A human without shame is like a meal without salt; a body without conation is like an ownerless slave".

Oruc Bey had a diet which he applied very strictly. He never ate tomatoes, potatoes or aubergines. Scallions were also added to the diet below because they cause flatulence. He recommended abstaining from sea food, with the exception of seaweed. Similarly, because of the mercury they contain and their fast deterioration rate, he did not eat fish. He avoided processed foods, packaged foods and goods that had been wrapped in nylon. He drank weak tea. When I first met him, he used a sweetener called Dulcaryl, which you could buy at pharmacies, but he later quit this and turned to honey. Honey was used for a long time, then molasses was used interchangeably. In the end, he started using a molasses type of sherbet that is obtained from a Central American cactus called Agave. All aluminum cookware was replaced by stainless steel utensils. He would only buy yogurt if it was prepared and sold in a heated pot and never used yogurt that was sold in plastic packaging. When making a choice, he would check whether the product contained any poisons or caused any diseases. He used to say that the main cause of modern diseases, such as MS, Alzheimer's Disease and Parkinson's Disease, was salts containing

---

31 In the following sections more information will be given about the Sufi Tour.

aluminum silicate. He believed that aluminum silicate, which is added to salt to make it pour, was a trigger for these diseases. He was very careful to eat meat that was Halal[32] and would not eat it if he had any doubts. In the early days of our acquaintance, he told me that he had fallen ill after eating meat that was not Halal and that a few days later the Directorate of Religious Affairs had issued a warning about Halal slaughter. All this happened in the 70s. While in Kadirga, they used sunflower seed oil, but soon afterwards went back to Extra Virgin Olive Oil and never used any other cooking oil. They never consumed margarine, preferring butter instead. He used to eat cream. The diet that he applied can be found below:

Recommended Foods

Lentils: Contain a substance called Dopamine, which develops brain cells. Lentil soup should be eaten everyday if possible.

Dates: Nutritional; contains no toxins.

Figs: They are even good for cancer. They clean the blood, remove toxins and reduce inflammation.

Olives: Leave no toxins in the intestines.

Weak tea: Weak and fresh tea can be consumed after meals.

Watermelons: Mevlevites eat these a lot.

Pomegranates: They have curing attributes.

Pumpkins or squash: Good for the stomach.

Turnips and carrots: They have antiseptic qualities and are full of vitamins (serve as an antidote to potatoes and tomatoes).

Broad beans: Good for the eyes.

Cabbage: Contains nitrogen; good for the stomach and the legs.

Mutton: Closest meat to human flesh. (Eat the part of the sheep that corresponds to the location of ailment – a direct quote from the Prophet (mPbuH).)

Parsley: Very beneficial for the stomach

Sage: Good for diabetes, refreshing.

Turmeric: Good for the respiratory tract

---

32 Meat slaughtered in accordance with Islamic guidelines

Ginger: Helps relieve gas; refreshing.

Galingale (related to ginger): Warms the blood

Thyme/Oregano: Good for influenza and common colds

Not recommended Foods

Fish and sea food: Contain no life energy; start to decompose as soon as they are caught and cause rotting in the intestines. Mystics (Evliyaullah) never eat fish.

Tomatoes-Potatoes-Aubergines-Tobacco: They contain a very strong poison called Solanine, which destroys body resistance, weakens willpower and can cause cancer and ulcers.

Spinach: Causes stones in the kidneys.

Bananas: Difficult to digest

Peaches: Exhaust the liver; have allergenic properties .

Fried foods: Exhaust the liver and stomach.

Margarines: They do not melt at body temperature; harmful, sometimes contain lard.

Cocoa or Chocolate: Destroys calcium in the body. Creates addiction and fatigues the mind.

Salt: Very little is sufficient for the body. Excess salt destroys Potassium, Fluorine and Bromine.

Hard-boiled Eggs: Very difficult to digest

Cakes: Cause headaches; usually contain margarine.

Aluminum cookware: Aluminum cannot be discharged from the body once it has been ingested. Destroys resistance. Causes cancer and ulcers and is known to accumulate in the brain.

Sausages (garlic sausage) - pastrami - spices: Cause liver fatigue and disorder in the stomach and intestines. Contain urea and sodium nitrate.

Coffee: Causes stomach disorder and palpitations.

One last thing that I would like to add is Oruc Bey's explanation of flu and the common cold. According to Oruc Bey, the common cold or flu are illnesses created by the human body in order to clean out the phlegm that forms inside the body and needs to be discharged. Phlegm consists mainly of dead body cells and other dischargeable residues. That is why in Turkish when you catch the flu or the cold you say, 'I've got the cure!'. I believe this approach to be the Transoxiana approach to medicine, which developed in the middle ages. You can prevent flu with vaccinations yet, when phlegm accumulates in the body and is not discharged, it may cause more dangerous diseases. Kindly take this as a serious note.

ORUC BEY AND MUSIC

Oruc Bey's introduction to music came about following a dream. I heard him relate this dream about twenty times on different occasions. But as we will see later in the 'Sohbet Manners' section, when Oruc Bey told a story he would adapt it to either the topic in hand or to the collective consciousness of the people present. That is why in each of his iterations, the story was either altered or certain sections of the story were removed. I present here two versions of this dream (information about the sources is in the footnotes).

Version One:

"Oruc Bey has a dream at the age of twelve years, in which a tall man in an overcoat hands him a violin and asks him to play. Oruc replies, 'I don't know how to play'. But the man insists, saying, 'You can play', whereupon Oruc Bey takes the violin and starts playing. According to Oruc Bey, it turns out to be a very good performance and he enjoys it very much. The next day, he tells this dream to his father, who takes him to a watchmaker called Turhan Agabey and explains that they are looking for a violin for Oruc. Turhan Agabey says that he has just one violin, which he plays himself. In those days, Tavsanli had a population of 15 thousand and only two people played the violin. However, Cevat Agabey, who works in the same shop, says that he has the very violin for Oruc Bey. This violin has its own story too. When a friend of Cevat Agabey was in Korea during the Korean war, one of his soldier friends gave him a violin as a present. He brought the violin back to Turkey but, since he did not know how to play it, he gave it to Cevat Agabey as a present. Cevat Agabey asks for the violin to be brought to the shop and sells it at a very affordable price. This violin is a three-quarter size Suzuki violin, suitable for children and, according to our source, is still being preserved. Oruc Bey receives violin lessons for three years from Fethi Bey, who is a very high class symphony orchestral musician. Oruc Bey's elder brother Yasar Guvenc also takes Mandolin lessons from the same person for three years.

"Oruc Bey attends the newly established Turkish Music Association in Tavsanli and later on goes to Istanbul for his University education. He works in some casinos for a short time, during which he learns how to play the qanun from an expert, who also develops his knowledge of Turkish tonalities and Turkish percussive rhythms. At the same time, Oruc Bey opens a music shop on Azimkar street in Laleli and starts giving music lessons himself. He also buys a tanbur from Hadi Usta and starts learning this instrument too. Prior to this, he had learned to play the rebab from Shemsettin Agabey (son of His Holiness Fazyl Bey) and the ney from Erdogan Agabey at the Tavsanli Turkish Music Association.[33]"

Oruc Bey with the first Rebab he made Infront of his Music Shop at Azimkar Street in Laleli.

Version Two:

"I was born in 1948. One night, sometime after 1960, I had a dream in which a tall, genial man, whom I did not know, handed me a violin. He was aged between forty-five and fifty and wearing a brown- or khaki-coloured coat. I genuinely did not know how to play the violin, but the gentleman told me that I could do it. I took the violin and began to play. I enjoyed it immensely and still remember the piece I played in my dream. It was a very good performance.

In the morning I told my dream to my father, who at the time was a journalist and publisher in the Tavsanli township of Kutahya. He listened to my dream but said nothing. Around noon, he told me to follow him and we went out together. In his youth, my father had worked as an apprentice in a watchmaker's shop. We went to the shop of the son of my father's master, the late Turhan Agabey, who used to play the violin. "We're looking for a violin for Oruc," said my father. Turhan Agabey

33 Source: Yasar Guvenc

replied, "I have a violin, but I am playing it myself, Kamil Agabey."
Cevat Agabey, who worked in the shop with Turhan Agabey, said
that he had the very violin for Oruc Bey and had the violin brought
from his home (another version of this story says that he fetched
the violin himself). It was a Suzuki three-quarter size violin suitable
for children aged twelve to fifteen. This violin also had a story. One
of Cevat Bey's friends had bought this violin in Japan when he was
away fighting in the Korean War. He brought it back with him to
his home in Erzurum and gave it to Cevat Bey when he visited him,
saying, "You play the saz, so maybe this violin will be of some use
to you." The violin had remained on the shelf in Cevat Bey's house
ever since. My father bought the violin for a very small amount and,
a few days later, we went to see Fethi Akuz, who was a music teacher
at the Tavsanli Middle School. He agreed to give lessons to me and
started me off with the German Hoffman method. I continued to
receive instruction from Fethi Bey for three years until the Turkish
Music Association opened in Tavsanli. Here, having learned musical
notations from Fethi Bey, I went on to develop my musical knowledge and study the tonalities of Turkish Music. We first fasyl[34] we
performed was the the Mahur fasyl."[35]

I would just like to add a humorous clip I came across while surfing
the internet some time ago. I should add that this link no longer exists.
Oruc Bey was being interviewed by a journalist, who asked which musical
instrument Oruc Bey played. The journalist obviously expected him to say
that he played the guitar, the oud and perhaps the bowed tanbur. However,
Oruc Bey amused the journalist by replying, "I play wind instruments,
bowed instruments, percussion instruments and plucked stringed instruments.!"

Since I also witnessed Oruc Bey playing the harmonium and the xylo-
phone, it would not have been incorrect if he had added, "I play keyboard
instruments too."

THE DONUSHUM (TRANSFORMATION) MUSIC GROUP

In the early 70s, Oruc Bey discovered the Donusum Group, founded by

---

34 Fasyl means a performance of different musical forms of a certain makam (tonality); in this case
   the Mahur tonality
35 http://www.gonuldergisi.com/muzigin-tedavi-gucu-rahmi-oruc-guvenc.html

Halit Kakinc and Muhtar Turan, through the Hey Magazine[36]. When Oruc Bey joined the group, it changed its name to 'The Donusum Folk Trio' and later, when Atilla Hunal joined them, their name changed again to 'Donusum Folk Quartet'. Oruc Bay laid down one condition for participation in this group, which was abstinence from any electronic music. In this group, Oruc Bey played the ney, the rebab, the kudum and the tar[37].

This group released 3 records in one year, which were: 'Kiziroglu Mustafa Bey', 'Seyyid Osman' and 'Kyzyl Yrmak'. Inspired by Oruc Bey, the

Group Donusum

group members used ancient Turkish musical instruments such as the tar and the jaw harp[38]. Their records ranked highly in lists of record sales at that time. The lyrics of 'Seyyid Osman' were in the Tatar dialect. This and other similar groups formed the basis of the National Music/Anatolian Folk Movement. Turkish people found this music contained characteristics and elements of their own culture, unlike the popularized musical

36 A very famous music magazinne published in the 70s in Turkey
37 Turkish musical instruments with Central Asian origins
38 A Turkic musical instrument; original name is the mouth or the jaw harp (agiz kopuzu, shan kopuz)

arrangements of the time [39].

The Department of Foreign Affairs and Culture arranged for the Donushum Group to visit Central Asia. On this tour they visited the republics of Turkmenistan, Kazakhstan, Uzbekistan, Kyrgyzstan, Tajikistan, Tataristan and Azerbaijan, all of which were part of the Soviet Union at the time. Oruc Bey was very much influenced by the things he saw there. He established a museum of musical instruments in Istanbul after being inspired by the Museum of Musical Instruments in Kazakhstan, where he saw over 300 exhibits of musical instruments.

Here, I want to relate three stories that I heard from Oruc Bey which, to my knowledge, have not been published anywhere before.

But first, I want to recap the political situation at the time. These were times before the breakup of the Eastern Bloc, when Central Asian Turks were all under communist rule and relations between the two blocs were tense. It was nearly impossible for an ordinary traveler to journey from one bloc to the other.

I have heard a lot of stories directly from Oruc Bey about journeys he made in those times. According to him, they were under

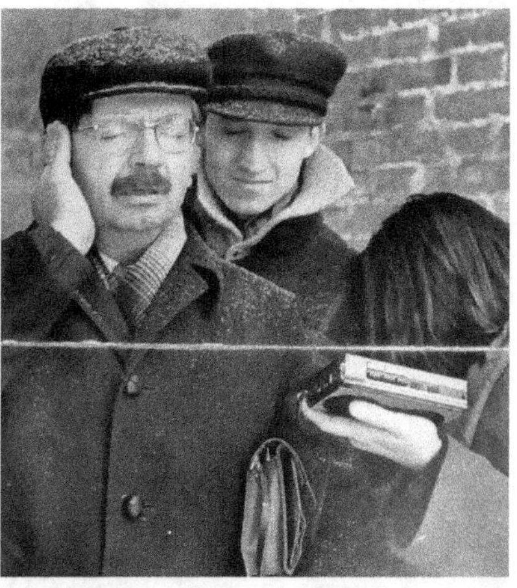

Yasar Guvenc chanting the Call for Prayer (Ezan) at The Minaret of Suyumbike in Tataristan

surveillance by guards at all times. Wherever they went, a couple of Soviet officers would be instructed to accompany them. However, on one occasion Oruc Bey somehow managed to evade the guards and slip through a small door into to a garden with a coffeehouse where he chatted with people and learned a multitude of things about the culture and music of the region.

While on this subject, I want to narrate the following story about a Central Asian woman (a Kazakh from East Turkestan) that I heard directly from Oruc Bey again.

One day they visited the house of a lady known locally in Istanbul as a

___

39 Arrangments that were basically foreign melodies with Turkish lyrics.

Baksy (Shaman). The lady performed a Shamanic ritual, during which she declared that one of the men there had a child. This person was known to be a bachelor who had never married. When the lady made this declaration, the man jumped up with his hand raised and shouted, "A lie!". But later, the man went up to Oruc Bey when he was alone and confessed that he did have a child.

Oruc Bey described the ritual as follows:

"After the ritual started, a chest suddenly appeared in a corner of the house. Soon afterwards, animals started emerging from the chest and began wandering about. Nobody else in our group saw those animals but me. Later, when I told the lady what I had seen, she said that she had been performing that ritual for 40 years and I was the only one to report seeing them until now."

According to Oruc Bey, the chest was a gift from the lady's Master. When he told me this story, I remembered a picture of a shamanic ritual that was engraved on a metallic surface, which I had seen in the English edition of the History Volume of the Meydan Larousse Encyclopedia. I searched through the encyclopedias for that picture for days without finding it until, forty years later, when I saw it while surfing through the Ancient Origins website. (http://www.ancient-origins.net/). The picture on this this website shows a visual reconstruction of an image of a Finno-Ugaric shaman, for which we possess the copyright. Note the similarities with the details in Oruc Bey's story.

Another story I want narrate took place at the end of a Tumata Concert in one of the Soviet Republics. After the concert, some speeches were being made on stage when suddenly a lady musician called Tamara took to the floor saying, "How long will it be before the Turks living in Turkey come to rescue us?". Nationalist feelings ran rampant and everyone in the theatre started crying. People got up and hugged each other. Thankfully, the Soviet Union was dissolved in December 1991. What had triggered this was the revolt staged by Kazakhs in the December (Jeltoksan) of 1991. This revolt spread rapidly to other republics and, one by one, all the Turkic Republics declared their independence, apart from those republics which were sparsely populated by Turks and which remain part of the Russian Federation today.

The other story that I heard took place in Dushenbe, capital of Tajikistan, in the late 70s or early 80s. I had listened to a radio program featuring an Azerbaijani music group, during which the Azerbaijani singer Leyla Sherifi sent greetings to the Turkish nation, saying, "I come from my country bringing words of friendship and brotherhood to my Turkish brothers and sisters..." In a conversation with Oruc Bey around that time, I mentioned the expressive beauty of this greeting, whereupon he told me a story about when they were in Dushenbe. The Turkish contingency had been wandering around a part of the city that was frequented by local Tajiks. When one of them realized that this group was from Turkey, he began reciting a long and emotional ode (gazel). All the locals gathered around to listen to this ode, which both impressed and moved Oruc Bey. He subsequently introduced the practice of occasionally reciting odes (gazels) during the Tumata Ensemble's Tuesday rehearsals.

Finno-Ugoric Shaman's Ritual

The Donusum Group did not release any more records after 1975, when it split up.

TUMATA GROUP

After these journeys and the musical experiences mentioned above Oruc Bey decided to research the traditional Turkic music of Central Asia and the musical instruments, costumes stage props and designs used for performance and to compile them in order to put on musical performances in Turkey. If I am not mistaken, it was around the time that he graduated from the Philosophy Department of Istanbul University. For this compilation and research mission, he formed a music group of performers and experts in dance and music. In 1975-76, this group operated under the name "The Group for the Research and Promotion of Turkish Music Group".

I must not omit a story that I heard a few times, which explains the origin of the name "TUMATA". When the ensemble started its activities as the 'Research and Promotion of Turkish Music Group', a close friend of Oruc Bey, the Journalist Iskender Bey, commented that the group's name was too long and that it would be difficult to gain recognition with that name. He then came up with the name TUMATA, an acronym of the original Turkish name, and the group has henceforth been known as

'TUMATA'.

Oruc Bey used the name TUMATA for any concerts or activities that involved musical performance. When researching and compiling this material, his intention had been to revive and present it for its cultural, educational, spiritual and therapeutic values.

Once, in the early days of my acquaintance with Oruc Bey, I had gone to visit him, alone or with a friend of mine (I don't quite remember), in his office at the Cerrahpasa Faculty of Medicine. At that time, the TUMATA mission was still it its formation stage and Oruc Bey was very interested in pentatonic music as a result of his trips to Central Asia. Facilities like the internet and mobile phones were not available then of course, and television transmissions were still broadcast in black and white over a single channel. That day, I had found him hunched over his typewriter writing an article on pentatonic music. After greetings and a short exchange of words, he showed me what he had written, which as I said was about pentatonic music. He confided in me that God had originally given pentatonic music to all the nations of the world. This music was a gift from God to all the peoples of the world.

TUMATA Ensemble during a performance

MUSIC THERAPY

During a visit to the second-hand bookstore in Bejazit around this time, Oruc Bey discovered a long article on Maqam music and Turkish music therapy in an old volume of the Hashim Bey Magazines[40]. He learned a great deal from this magazine article, which contained many illustrations, and music therapy, which had remained at the back of his mind, now emerged to become the core of the scientific research to be carried out in this domain. I can categorically state that the person responsible for reviving the tradition of Turkish music therapy was Rahmi Oruc Guvenc. Had it not been for his work on this subject, it would have been accorded no more than short passages and footnotes in a few scientific books that remained unread or even known about. I am not saying that no one but him

40 A very old magazine published in the early years of the Turkish Republic.

was aware of this subject. Throughout history, we have had other great scholars who were experts in this field. But I emphasize that the person who revived all the dimensions of traditional Turkish music therapy for use in modern medicine was Assistant Professor Dr. Rahmi Oruc Guvenc.

Many of the short biographical works On Oruc Bey found by surfing the internet state that Oruc Bey completed his Doctorate in 1986. However, the first page of his doctoral indicates that it was submitted in 1985. In of those days when there was no computerized infrastructure, it can be surmised that acceptance of the thesis and completion of the paperwork might have taken some time. The title of the thesis was 'The History and Current Status of Mental Therapy through Music in Turkey and the World'. The sixth section, headed 'Summary', contains the following passage:

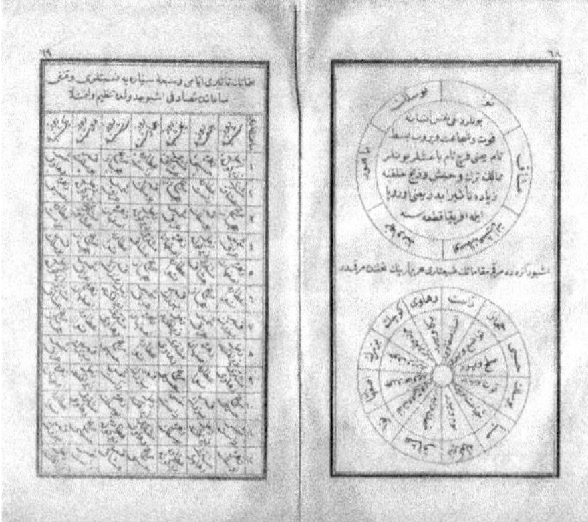

Images from the Hashim Bey Magazine

"This study discussed the history and current situation of mental therapy through music in Turkey and the World. It illustrated that music is an important phenomenon in human societies, which has an direct or indirect effect on the behavior and thought processes of individuals in society.

"Mental therapy through music is a method known to have been used since ancient times. This system, which originated in Central Asia, was perfected in the Seljuk and Ottoman eras.

"This study showed how, when four types of music sessions were applied to 22 patients who had come from a polyclinic with anxiety neuroses, it was found that there were changes in their psychogalvanic response levels and an increase in their skin resistance. It was also observed that patients benefited most from gentle improvisations on simple Japanese pentatonic melodies played on the ney. The positive effects on anxiety brought about by music was consistent with similar recorded research.

"It was also noted that emphasis is placed on the use of music in the treatment of mental illnesses in hospitals throughout the world."

When Dr. Rahmi Oruc Guvenc completed his clinical psychology doctorate in music therapy under the tutelage of Prof. Dr. Ayhan Songar, he became the only expert in this field and soon afterwards was promoted to the position of Assistant Professor by the intercollegiate board on the grounds of his studies into the therapeutic values of Turkish Music and its place in the world music, his work on promoting, manufacturing, repairing and teaching Turkish musical instruments.

THE BEGINNING OF ORUC BEY'S CONNECTIONS WITH EUROPE

As I said before I met Oruc Bey in the late 1970s or early 1980s and had the privilege of attending many of his sohbets at his house in Kadirga. The first foreigner I met there was an Austrian gentleman who was working on children with behavioral disorders. But Oruc Bey and his close companions had already met the person who was going to put them in contact with Europe, but I knew nothing of this at the time. According to copyright laws, I would need their personal permission to use their real names, so I will use nicknames. Thus, I will call this person Amadeus. There are two versions of the story about Oruc Bey's acquaintance with Europe through Mr. Amadeus. The first is as follows:

When Mr. Amadeus was in his thirties, he had a friend who was a student of George Gurdjieff. What I mean is that he was introduced to Sufism through this friend. Mr. Amadeus had always wanted to meet dervishes but, since he was living in Vienna, thought there was no chance of this happening. Around this time, he had also read a book on the effects of sound.

One day, when sitting in a street somewhere, a man passed by who aroused the curiosity of Mr. Amadeus, who consulted his friends, gave them a description of the man, and asked for his name and address. His friends told him they would make investigations and finally found out who he was. This person was a famous painter. Mr. Amadeus obtained his address and went to visit him in the outskirts of Vienna. Within a very short time, they became good friends. This painter, who was of Turkish origin, had been living abroad since he was sixteen but, before leaving home, he had had a dream about Ibn al-Arabi[41] and was following the path of this order.

The painter invited Amadeus and his wife to Istanbul, where he met Oruc Bey for the first time. Amadeus stated that he felt a resonance the moment he met Oruc Bey, who invited them to a musical event. Mr. Amadeus said that, on arrival at the venue, he saw there were only two vacant seats remaining. He sat on one of them and his wife on the other.

In return, Mr. Amadeus invited Oruc Bey to a folk music festival in Bregenz and it was after this that Oruc Bey's interaction with Europe began in earnest.

The other version of this story is as follows:

Mr. Amadeus was a guitar teacher at a conservatory in Bregenz, Austria. He went to see a friend of his in Linz in 1979 or 1980. At this friend's house, he saw a book on Sufism lying on a table. He looked through the book and was fascinated by the topics it contained.

One day, while walking down a street, he had a sudden urge to ring the bell of a house that he knew nothing about. He rang the bell. It so happened that a painter of Turkish origin lived there. The painter invited Mr. Amadeus in without any hesitation and they engaged in a deep conversation on Sufism, for which Mr. Amadeus was already prepared for he had read a book on Ibn al-Arabi a few days earlier. The painter invited Mr. Amadeus to Turkey, where his brother was the percussion player in the TUMATA Ensemble. This was how Mr. Amadeus became acquainted with Oruc Bey. Mr. Amadeus presented Oruc Bey with a shakuhachi (a Japanese flute made from bamboo) as a present and in return Oruc Bey gave him a ney. Mr. Amadeus became very interested in Oruc Bey's work and invited him to a folk music festival in Bregenz, followed by performances at

---

41 A great Arabian Mystic who lived in the Middle Ages.

Garmisch-Patenkirchen, Innsbruck and Vienna, while their friendship developed further.

I would like to add one other thing to this story, which is that every summer since they met (in 1980, to be exact), Mr. Amadeus would invite Oruc Bey and his group as his guests to Torronteras, a small town near Madrid. After the departure of Oruc Bey's physical presence from this earth, Mr. Amadeus continued this tradition by inviting Yasar Guvenc and his group to go and play there. They would end their stay with a 'fiesta' on the last day.

CENTRES, SCHOOLS IN EUROPE, AND OTHER ACTIVITIES

In 1990, Oruc Bey together with a theologist and a psychologist called Gerhard Kadir Tucek founded the Schule fur Altorientalische Musik und Kunsttherapie in Schloss Rosenau, Austria, with a curriculum based on the Turkish music therapy tradition. The first graduates of this school received their diplomas in October 1995 at a concert performance organized jointly by Trakya University and Istanbul Technical University's Turkish Music State Conservatory at the Bajezid II Hospital (Shifahane) in Edirne.

Oruc Guvenc had studied the history, culture and music of Turkic communities living in various parts of the world and, apart from this school in Schloss Rosenau, he established centres in Almaty, Bishkek, Vienna, Rosenau, Frankfurt, Hamburg, Munich, Freiburg, Zurich, Brussels and Barcelona in order to further these studies. A Turkish Music Therapy pilot project was started with the joint cooperation of Marmara University, the Rosenau Music Therapy School and the Munich University's Music Academy. In addition, music therapy schools were opened in Germany (Berlin and Mannheim), Switzerland (Zurich) and Spain (Barcelona and Madrid) and they are currently still in operation. Istanbul University, the school in Austria and Vienna University have jointly organized three music therapy and ethnomusicology symposia and two ethnomusicology music festivals.

Assistant Professor Dr. Rahmi Oruc Guvenc also published a book called 'Turkish Music History and Turkish Therapeutic Music', containing detailed information on pentatonic music, Medieval Turkish Hospitals (Shifahane), the therapeutic value of Turkish Music and Turkish music in general, plus many compositions, with notation, from the Turkic World.

Oruc Bey started his clinical studies into music therapy in 1993. He completed the neurology studies that began at the Meidling Clinic in Vienna and, has been carrying out studies into cardiology since 2000 and oncology studies since 2001. He had also begun work on the disabled in 1993. Other than these, some projects on geriatrics and immunology that were started in collaboration with Oruc Bey are still ongoing. Oruc Guvenc conducted a study on 'pain' with Prof. Dr. Avni Babacan at Gazi University's Algology Department and he conducted some scientific studies on chemotherapy patients at Ankara Numune Hospital.

ISTANBUL UNIVERSITY ETHNOMUSICOLOGY RESEARCH AND APPLICATION CENTER

I.U Ethnomusicology Research and Application Centre was founded on 05 September 1991 and Assistant Professor Rahmi Oruc Guvenc was appointed as its artistic director and a board member. Between 1994 and 1995 I had the opportunity of helping him with his work for about a year. He had asked me to translate a book written by Juliette Alvin entitled 'Music Therapy for the Autistic Child', which I remember translating within two or three months. Rahmi Oruc Guvenc held this position until 1995, when he was appointed as a lecturer at Marmara University's Institute of Turkology, from where he retired in 2004.

Some images from Oruc Bey's book

FRIENDSHIP BRIDGE FESTIVALS, FROM THE HEART TO MEDICINE FROM MEDICINE TO THE HEART SYMPOSIA AND VOICES OF LIGHT CONCERTS

Oruc Bey and his ensemble organized or participated in countless concerts, festivals, conferences, symposia, events, workshops, music and instrument classes and talk programs. You can find information about these over the internet on a date, country or city basis; instead of showering you with details, here I would like to inform you about three of their most prominent activities. The first is Friendship Bridge Festival. It has been staged in many countries and it is based on the principle of staging musical performances of different countries within the same organization. Again, for a better understanding of the subject would like to cite the following lines which Oruc Bey wanted me to translate at around those times:

"The holy and the healing sounds of the East and the West form the language of society and the heart. The Friendship Bridge project was started in 1993 and is being resumed by Dr. Rahmi Oruc Guvenc who happens to be an ethnomusicology, a music therapist and a Master of Music-Sufism connections. The idea of presenting different musical traditions and dances as an application of art on the stage belongs to Dr. Guvenc. The roots of his traditions have directed him to form bridges from the Far East to the Far West.

The Friendship Bridge project has been carried out since 1993, in various places and different times in Turkey and Europe by a variety of performers and therapists in, for example, Istanbul, Ankara, Zurich, Basel, Munich, Hamburg, Salzburg, Vienna, Madrid, Barcelona, Brussels, Berlin, Nevsehir and Urgup.

Bridges allow us to live as a cultural fraternity of different beliefs, lifestyles and experiences that are far from each other.

The aim of the Friendship Bridge project is to experience the tolerance and the Climate of Friendship while preserving originality. Music which is a nonverbal mean of expression that allows us to breath in comfort and tranquility, is also a language that forms in the heart and reaches other hearts and is felt throughout the universe.

It aims to form feelings of joy and good and pleasant desires, dances, songs, friendship, love, compassion, gratitude, ascription, humbleness, generosity. In the performances archaic Baksy melodies and artistic and spiritual folklore tunes are being presented. Music and dance have been applied in the world for thousands of years and particularly its equilibrating attributes for the body and the mind are utilized."[42]

FROM HEART TO MEDICINE AND FROM MEDICINE TO HEART SYMPOSIA

From the Heart to Medicine and From Medicine to Heart Symposium

42 Friendship Bridge Festival - https://tumata.com/faaliyetler/dostluk-koprusu-festivali/

At the beginning and in the medical developments in the Transoxiana[43] culture, the prevalent idea was that health was acquired through the unity and the equilibrium of the body and the mind. But as time passed medicine became an area of research and application gravitating to the body only. Although areas of science like psychology, psychiatry and pedagogy matured, the human possibilities which were in broad sense open to infinite knowledge and infinite perception were neglected.

Particularly in the 20th century medicine realized its deficiencies in these areas and opted to compensate.

In order to evaluate all the acquired information under current conditions and to reach a summary of these historical works and developments we have been organizing the "From Medicine to the Heart, From the Heart to Medicine - Preparation for the Future Seminars" since 2005.

Asst. Prof. Dr. Rahmi Oruc Guvenc

REGENERATIVE MEDICINE AND SPIRITUALITY

Regenerative Medicine (Latin, regeneration: to regenerate, to rejuvenate) is a new and a valid area in biological medicine. This new area of science accepts in principle the fact that cells, tissues and organs which have deteriorated in function recover from various diseases through regeneration and one of its points of emphasis is the activation of the intrinsic regeneration and repair processes in a living entity.

Under the light of this basic knowledge, the aspect of conscience use of patients' bodily potential in terms of healing has gained great actuality in the world of medicine. In this sense, beginning with the diagnosis talk (anamnesis) with the patient, taking into consideration the rhythmic cell processes which are regulatory time processes, gradually play a greater role in treatment recommendations. Accordingly, a very wide angle comes into question ranging from the use of neo-psychotherapy and cell biology to ancient oriental music, Sufi music and Central Asian pentatonic music which is represented hon-

---

43 Area conjointly occupied in our day by Turkmenistan, Kazkhstan and Uzbekistan also known as Khorasan

orably by Dr. Oruc Guvenc.

Ulrich Randoll MD[44]

"The Voices of Light" programs were other activities which consisted of performances where authentic instruments and authentic repertories were performed. Again, they were held in various countries and cities and drew great attention in our country and abroad. [45]

YASAR GUVENC, OTAG MUSIC CENTER AND THE MUSEUM

In reality Oruc Bey has two other brothers: Yasar Guvenc who is an agricultural engineer (his elder brother) and his younger brother Nejat Guvenc who worked as a pilot for many years. Yasar Guvenc participated intensively in Oruc Bey's activities and supported him with every means possible. Just like Oruc Bey he plays various instruments. Yasar Guvenc whom I happened know very closely retired in 1994 and opened Otag Music Center. The shop changed its address a few times and finally moved to its present place at Alaykosku Avenue. While I was conversing with Yasar Guvenc (Yasar Agabey) about the book I told him that there was no information about him and asked him whether he could supply me with some information about himself and he was courteous enough to hand me over a single page biography which he once personally put into words. The biography given to me by Yasar Guvenc who happens to be my other benefactor is as follows:

"He was born in Tavsanli in 1945, the first child of Ahmet Kamil and Urkiye Guvenc. While he completed Istiklal Primary School and Tavsanli Middle School in Tavsanli he finished High School in Kutahya. He served as a Vocational Lessons teacher in the Konya/ Konuklar Agricultural Vocational School following his graduation as an agricultural engineer from Ankara Agricultural Faculty in 1969. Later on he took office at Eskisehir Technical Agricultural Directorate and Istanbul Provincial Agricultural Directorate. For a while he served as a Projects and Statistics Branch Director. He retired in 1994 and opened Otag Music Center. He began his music life by taking mandolin lessons from Fethi Bey when he was in middle school. He learned how to play the Saz during High School and the Ney and

44 https://tumata.com/faaliyetler/kalpten-tibba-tiptan-kalbe-sempozyumu/
45 TUMATA mesmerized the residents of Munich Ahttp://www.munihinsesi.com/haber-4034-tumeta_munihe_geliyor.html

the Jumbus during his university years. Later on he began to play the Rebab, Tanbur and the Oud. Nowadays he is developing his abilities in playing the Shiraz Tar and he is continuing his music and music therapy activities in TUMATA Music Group led by his brother Rahmi Oruc Guvenc.

He is engaged in the production and the trade of musical instruments, cassettes, CDs and souvenirs at Otag Music Center which he opened following his retirement. He won the first place prize with his composition (Hu Allah) in the Yunus Emre Hymns composition contest sponsored by the Eskisehir Cultural Directorate in 1975. Also he composed the poem (Yar Yuregim Yar) written also by Yunus Emre."

Yasar Guvenc

TUMATA Center is located in a close vicinity of the Otag Music Center which was established by Yasar Guvenc. The 2 floor center is located in the 3rd and 4th floors of the building in question. While the upper floor is a place where Tuesday rehearsals of TUMATA are held, the lower floor is a place comprising the kitchen and other rooms where plaquets, plates, awards and similar artifacts awarded to Oruc Bey are exhibited. At the upper floor and partially in the lower floor in some glass partitions one can find exhibits of musical instruments pertaining to the Turkic World and the World culture in general. In other words the upper floor in fact is a museum.

Oruc Bey tells us how he reached the idea of forming a museum as follows:

"The oldest material within the music therapy tradition of Turkish Music is the pentatonic music. Today there are many obsolete instruments that were used in making this music. If we look at Anatolia we can mention 30-35 musical instruments at the most. This includes

Military Music, Classical Turkish Music, Sufi Music, Frontier Songs and folklore music. In Almaty/Kazakhstan I saw more than 400 instruments in a museum. In our museum in Istanbul we gathered more than 300 musical instruments belonging to the Turkic World. The fact of the matter is that we have thousands of musical instruments. But no one is aware of this. This is overt disloyalty. I think it is a deficiency not to have these taught in schools."[46]

I remember Oruc Bey mentioning a concept he called "A Live Museum" in conversations we held in the past. His idea was a museum where a person could take the instrument and, examine and if I may say so twangle it a bit; and he had accomplished this at the TUMATA CENTER. In 2017 while watching a Kazakh TV channel I saw a mechanism where one could play the tune in the provided list with authentic Turkic instruments of your choice thanks to the computer infrastructure installed at the museum; and I had liked this very much. Shortly before his passing Oruc Bey and Master instrument maker Feridun Obul supplied many instruments to the Anatolian University for a musical instruments museum and contributed greatly with their ideas.

OTAG MUSIC CENTER

Previously I had mentioned that Yasar Guvenc opened Otag Music Center in 1994 following his retirement. In this locality apart from musical instruments, CDs, books, various authentic make wares and many products for herbal use are being traded. The musical instruments can be own make as well as being brought from abroad. Dombras with Kazakh origin sold in the shop can be a good example to this. Apart from these in their own web site many music albums belonging to TUMATA and albums produced for TUMATA by foreign music groups are made available as MP3 downloadable products.

The web sites are as follows: otagmuzik.com, otagmusic.com

TUESDAY REHEARSALS

In the Tumata Center we mentioned before, music rehearsals are held on Tuesdays after 7 PM. This a longstanding Tumata tradition. Tea and red lentil soup are offered to the participants who come to watch and sing, and the music performances continue till 9 PM.

---

46 TRT Vizyon Dergisi, August 2017, No: 338, p. 15

THE AWARDS RECEIVED BY ORUC GUVENC

Due to his Sufi nature, Oruc Bey never gave too much importance to worldly honors and distinctions; however he had many awards and he exhibited them on the first floor of the Tumata Center. You can still see this exhibition on the 3rd floor (the 1st floor of the center) of the building where Tumata Center is located. In 1994 when we were together at the Cerrahpasa Ethnomusicology Center he had told me how he got the Professor Emeritus title from the Uzbek Science Delegation as follows: The delegation had liked the works of Oruc Bey very much and following a TUMATA concert in Istanbul they put the Professor Emeritus Title to the vote: All participants raised their hands in favor and thus in 1992 he received the Fergana University Professor Emeritus title from the Uzbek Science Delegation. Again in 1992 Oruc Bey was awarded the honorable mention of the Academia de las Naciones in Argentine. You can again see this award which consist of a certificate and a wooden tower like plaquet at the Tumata Center. Rahmi Oruc Guvenc who received a Thank You and an Achievement prize (1993) from Boston Massachusetts University (US) was also awarded Motif Folklore Training Association's outstanding service award in the music research area in 1996. He received the Outstanding Service to the Turkic World Award from TURKSAV in 2004. And lastly, Oruc Guvenc received the 'Red Apple' Culture Award in 2016.

Views from Otag Music Center

Apart from these in 1998 between 24-28 of February at the "Friendship Song Contest" in the city of Neftkamsk in Baskurtistan which is a confederate of the Russian Federation TUMATA ensemble headed by Rahmi Oruc Guvenc received the 3rd place prize. The song that brought them the 3rd place prize was a song called "Dostlyk Jyry (Song of Friendship)" written in Tatar dialect with composition and lyrics by Oruc Bey. Here I find it appropriate to give the notation and the lyrics. According to Oruc Bey the song "Orenburg Shawl" which was again performed by the TUMATA ensemble was deemed to be the song that was the warmest and revived the feelings of friendship the best according to the selection board.

SUFI TOUR

Another tradition that Oruc Bey and his group resumed was the Sufi Tour activity. I would like to state that I participated in this tour with Oruc Bey in 1994. This tour is more like a spiritual journey and is an activity where Great Mystics within the Turkish geography are visited. During the trip when appropriate Oruc Bey gave historical and spiritual information about the location reached, and the information was translated and shared among the participants. During

Asst. Prof. MD Rahmi Oruc Guvenc and the 'Red Apple Award'

the evenings at hotels and other accommodation areas talks (sohbets) were held related to emerging subjects and when possible music was also made. Following the passing (the physical departure) of Oruc Bey this tradition is resumed by his elder brother Yasar Guvenc.

Oruc Bey described the essence and the aim of the Sufi Tour with the following lines which he put into paper years ago and which I had the privilege of translating:

"When spiritual factors which constitute the structure of existence of the Turkish People reach harmony with physical-mundane material, it is seen that science, culture and art synthesis gains acceleration.

Turkish Sufism, which developed within the souls of Anatolian people and which has taken especially the Khorasan (Transoxiana) culture as a basis – within the integrity of Central Asia and Anatolia connection – has been lived by spiritual Masters like His Holiness Mevlana, His Holiness Hadji Bektash-i Velî, His Holiness Hadji Bayram-i Velî, His Holiness Uftade, His Holiness Emir Sultan, His Holiness Yunus Emre, His Holiness Niyazi Misri, His Holiness Karacaahmet Sultan, Her Holiness Gunes Hanim, Her Holiness Karyagdi Sultan, Her Holiness Kadincik Ana, etc... and their ways of living was reflected to humanity at large.

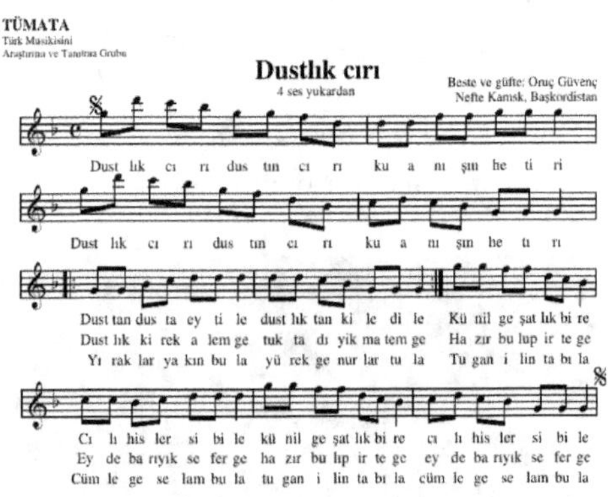

Dusttan dusta eytile
Dustlıktan kile dile
Künilge şatlık bire
Cılı hisler sibile

Dustlık cırı dustın cırı
Kuanışın hetırı

Dustlık kirek alemge
Tukta dıyik matemge
Hazır bulıp irtege
Eyde barıyık seferge

Dustlık cırı...

Yıraklar yakın bula
Yürekge nurlar tula
Tugan ilin tabıla
Cümlege selam bula

Dustlık cırı...

Song of Friendship, the Composition and the Lyrics

There are people who discover the true meanings of narrations by the Prophet Mohammed, such as, "Bona fide masters do not die, they change form", and "Die before death takes you". To visit them and remember them at their eternal resting place, to accept with respect the level of spiritual feelings they have reached, and to acquire examples from their moods, we are willing to repeat a spiritual tour, which has become a tradition for the last 14 years, between 11th and 23rd of December 2003.

Through this path we believe that the ego (nefs) will be disciplined in acknowledging that life continues after death and we believe that we will visit the reality that emanates within us and in the Great Mystics.

As it is stated in the book Tezkiretu'l-Evliya[47] written by the great Sufi Feriduddin-i Attar, in one narration The Prophet (mPbuH) had proclaimed that "Grace rains to places where Allah's friends are mentioned". By remembering them we put into words our wish to get acquainted with the grace and beneficence that has emanated to the manifested world at large and to breath in the meaning of unity that has emanated in the Great Mystics.

In one versicle of the Qoran it is said that "Allah's prosperity descends through the beneficent (people who give without expecting a return)". Clearly - according to our beliefs - the moods that emerge in the Mystics of Allah are moods like beneficence, mercy, love, sharing, and tolerance.

To allocate time for all of these we are carrying out this spiritual voyage as a tradition in the month of December since 1990.

Like the previous tours, there will be local and foreign participants and during the tour there will be concerts, conferences and conversations, and throughout our visits spiritual values will be felt and soul bonds will be formed.

Another aspect of the tour is the journey phenomenon. Prophet Mohammed's (mPbuH) narration: "Travel and find health" is an explicit guide in this respect.

The path to convert spiritual subjects from theory into practice, is to try to realize them in the mundane world. To unify oneself with the moods of Great Sufis at their spiritual abodes strengthens feelings of sincerity."

SEMA[48]

As I noted in various places before my aim in this book is to provide concise information about the life and the activities of Oruc Bey rather than engaging you with needless details like dates, places and times. That is why it wouldn't be appropriate if I don't mention the Sema activities which have been continuing since 2000. If you like let me cite directly from

47 Memoirs of the Mystics
48 Sema is the whirling activity of dervishes practiced to reach trance or alter their moods. The Sema activities of TUMATA on the other hand, are gatherings of all sufis from all around the world where sema activity never stops, semazens (whirling dervishes) take turns as well as the musicians so that sema and the whirling never stops for a previously allotted span of time.

Oruc Bey via an internet news portal:

"The thirtieth 3 days and nights Sema" activity organized by the Group for the Research and Promotion of Turkish Music (TUMATA) has begun in Termal/Yalova . Besides Turkish participants around 100 people coming from Germany, Iran, the US, Syria, Iraq and Switzerland will take part in the Sema activity which will last for 3 days and nights at the Rasim Mutlu Culture Center. The leader of the group Asst. Prof. Dr. Rahmi Oruc Guvenc has notified the journalist that His Holiness Mevlana had 3 times performed 40 days and nights Sema and many times 3 days and nights and 7 days and nights Sema. Mr. Guvenc who iterated that according to certain sources it has been cited that His Holiness Mevlana performed the Sema in 40 separate places at the same time, continued as follows: "Today when we examine these narrations we might become skeptical but we thought that we should try and see the facts in application. Around 15 years ago we started the 3 days and nights Sema program at a saloon in Zurich/Switzerland. His Holiness Mevlana performed this feat all by Himself, but we tried to carry it out with forty people and by sharing.

For 3 days and nights Sema, music and chanting never stopped. Musicians, Whirling dervishes and the chanters continued by interchanging and we managed to carry out the event. There were friends who started with 3-5 minutes whirling and developed this to 9-10 hours non-stop whirling."

Mr. Guvenc iterated that participants from all over the world came to Termal. Guvenc who told us that hundreds of people from 66 different countries took part in previous events continued as follows:

"The 3 days and nights Sema activity has been performed 29 times since its beginning. This is the thirtieth. Starting with Switzerland we continued with performances in 5 countries: Switzerland, Austria, Germany, Spain and Turkey. Apart from the 3 days and nights Sema, in this very same location 7 times 7 days and nights, 3 times 40 days and nights, once 66 days and nights and again once a 99 days and nights Sema activity was carried out. Last year, the 99 days Sema activity was carried out here. We have a wish to accomplish a sixteen days and nights Sema in August. "How many days and nights after these?" some friends ask. 99 days was a long time and thank God we carried it out without a hitch. The year 2016 may be a rest year. In 2017 we wish to hold a 114 days and nights Sema and slowly we are preparing our friends. The reason for this is that the number 114 is something like the number pi and it is also the number of the surahs in the Holy Quran. We want to try this also".

Guvenc drew attention to the fact that many people with different religious, vocational and sentimental backgrounds unite in the teachings of His Holiness Mevlana by participating in the Sema activities. Guvenc who drew attention to the importance of this fact said the following:

"The essence of this is based on knowledge and love and their side elements which are tolerance and sharing.

We think that all of these are sentiments and forms of behavior that people need. We think that such an establishment, such an application serves humanity suitably as a model."[49]

As described in the news excerpt the location for the Sema activities in Turkey, especially in long Sema programs happened to be the Mehmet Rasim Mutlu Culture Center. Firstly you may ask who on earth is Mehmet Rasim Mutlu; so let's start from there shall we? Mehmet Rasim Mutlu (Mutlu Baba) is a Sufi Master who devoted himself to the Sufi Path after quitting a very high yielding business life in the 70s. Mutlu Baba who founded the Sufistic Ideas Association presided as the head of the association for 20 years. Mutlu Baba who has many apprentices is at the same time a poet, a composer and an author who has put on paper many works.

His acquaintance with Oruc Bey's group took place during a Sufi Tour in the early 90s and Mutlu Baba and his group invited Oruc Bey and his companions to a musical sohbet environment at the hotel that they were staying. Since the paths and the hearts were on the same track the resonance survived to this date. At around the same time a Lady known as Havva Ana (Mother Eve) who was known to be very charitable donated a property she owns in Gokcedere to Mutlu Baba. Mutlu Baba planned to build a Dergah on this property but people who learned his intentions expressed their reservations saying that no one will ever come there. Mutlu Baba finished off the drawings of the octagon Dergah. Octagon structure is an architectural design form and many famous buildings embody this

49 3 days and nights Sema activity began in Termal, source: www.haber7.com, 03-04-2015

octagonal template. Interested parties can investigate this issue over the internet. One day when Mutlu Baba and his companions were working on the possible construction plans on the property site a turtle appeared among the digitaria and walked until it was between Mutlu Baba's feet and stopped there. Thereupon Mutlu Baba voiced his following foresight: "The Dergah will be completed but the construction will take a long time."

Personally I had the opportunity to participate in the 66, 99 and 114 days and nights Sema activities in this Dergah; the Dergah was visited by thousands of local and foreign enthusiasts. When I was putting these notes into paper, notifications were posted for 3 days and nights Sema activity in Hatay and 9 days and nights Sema activity in Gokcedere (March-2018).

A snapshot from the Sema Hall - Gokcedere/Yalova

At the entrance floor of the Dergah one can see the Abode of the Sheikh (Mutlu Baba) (far left), the Abode of Oruc Bey (in the center) and the abode of Yasar Guvenc (far right).

TALKS (SOHBETS)

I had previously mentioned that during the Sufi Tours sohbets and musical gatherings were held in the evenings. During the Sema activities sohbets were held especially following supper. During the month of Ramadan the sohbets of Oruc Bey began 45 minutes to 1 and a half hours before iftar[50] (breaking of the fast) and continued after a half hour interval following the iftar. During times other than the month of Ramadan he would usually ask for his famous attaché case and since usually I was the one present in the management room, I brought the case that was in the room to the area of sohbet at the entrance of the ground floor. The attaché case had a strange opening and closing mechanism and only Oruc Bey was in command of this issue. When you tried to open it one of the two locks on either of the two sides would not open and used to get stuck and Oruc Bey would make masterful strikes to arbitrary sections of the case and thus he would open and close it. As far as I remember it was more difficult close the case in comparison to opening it! When I asked for the content of the attaché case the daughter of Oruc Bey, E.B.Kanikey Guvenc-Akcay did not turn me down and sent me the following list:

The 6 volumes of the Masnavi of His Holiness Mevlana, Rebaba-name - His Holiness Sultan Veled, The Legends of the Enlightened Ones - Ahmet Eflâkî, Mevlevi Order after Mevlana - Abdulbaki Golpinarli (2 copies), The Door of Grace - His Holiness Kenan Rifai, Hymns in 99 Tonalities - Cuneyd Kosal, Hymns - Yapi Kredi Publishing - 1986, the Nectar of the Essence - His Holiness Ibn al-Arabî, The Daily Prayers of Mevlana - Rumi Publishing, The Mental Reasons of all Illnesses and Thought Models that Provide Healing - L. Louise, The Secret of the Secrets - His Holiness Abdulkadir Geylânî, News from the Beyond - Bahar Publishing, Tumata booklet (Turkish Music Therapy Tradition and Medicine - Tumata Practices), Tumata brochures and the Heritage Booklet of TUMATA and 1 pocket handkerchief.

Abodes (Dergah-Gokcedere)

---

50 The breaking of the fast in the month of Ramadan following sunset.

First thing that comes to mind in respect to this issue is that Oruc Bey always addressed the over-all level. He took care to address the collective consciousness of the audience throughout the sohbet duration. The other and maybe a more important issue was the spontaneous emergence of subjects and events (zuhurat). As Oruc Bey put it himself he took care to ' be at peace for what is at hand, and to be ready to engage in spontaneous emergences.' Generally for every sohbet there was a general title, however depending on the emerging factors either this general title was discussed or verged upon, or a digression was made.

For example once at the very early stages of one sohbet a lady from the audience asked a question like, " What is the meaning of life, why are we living?". As a reply Oruc Bey started his talk predominantly on "reaching the correct knowledge and living accordingly' and completed the sohbet touching also on the general title.

When appropriate, musical performances were also carried out to revive the mental mood of the audience and to create a pleasant atmosphere. Hymns and songs were voiced, musical improvisations were made and even odes (gazels) were vocalized. As I mentioned in the previous list there were three literary works that he always kept by his side and consulted often. These were the six volumes of the Masnavi, the Legends of the Enlightened Ones by Ahmed Eflaki and the Rebabname of His Holiness Sultan Veled. Here I don't want to leave out that Oruc Bey gave a special importance to the books Fususu'l-Hikem (the Nectar of Essence) by Ibn al-Arabî and A'mak-i Hayal (Depths of Imagination) by Ahmed Hilmi of Filibe (Plovdiv). During the sohbets enthusiasts who came to the Dergah from distant places or people who had carried out an important deed that day were asked to choose a number between 1 and 6 and a random page was opened from the Masnavi volume corresponding to the chosen number. In Islam this is called "tefe'ul" and this practice goes back to the times of our Prophet (mPbuH). It is a part of the tefe'ul to receive guidance, interpret favorably and to find solutions for problems from the things written in the opened page. The reverse portending (teshe'um) does not have place in Islam.

It was said by Ebu Hureyre (ra) that he had heard the Prophet (mPbuH) say, "There is no portent (teshe'um) in Islam, the best is to interpret favorably (tefe'ul)."[51]

Once an enthusiast who arrived only just from another continent was asked to pick a number between 1 and 6. In response that individual said '7'. Oruc Bey was prepared as always; in such circumstances he resorted to the Rebabname of the son of His Holiness Mevlana, Sultan Veled, which he always kept by his side with the six volumes of the Masnavi.

With no regard to books opened all sections were translated and for example in the case of the Masnavi a break was taken and the passages were read aloud by the speakers of the language from the German, the Spanish and the English translations.

When the Masnavi was opened sometimes one would encounter passages related to the character called Dakuki who had spiritual connections with the higher reality. Oruc Bey would radiate grace with short and long explanations where appropriate.

Following the sohbet, table zikr and similar practices were carried out, prayers, Salavat[52] and the surah of Fatiha[53] were read, and in the aftermath of these watermelon, entrements with tea or helvah[54] were served. Around this time Oruc Bey would go the Sema Hall upstairs and carry out a musical performance for approximately 2 hours. Collective zikr had an important place in the Sema Hall practices of Oruc Bey, and various zikr formations were formed under the active and standing guidance of Oruc Bey which took 45 minutes to intervals exceeding 1 and a half hours.

SOHBET CONTENTS

7TH OF JUNE 2017
(SOUND TRACK: STE038 - 114 DAYS SEMA ACTIVITY - DERGAH/GOKCEDERE)

In this sohbet Oruc Bey initially begins the talk with music therapy and indicates that music therapy and other associated elements developed under the name of 'Alternative Medicine' and finally were named as 'Complementary Medicine'. In another sohbet Oruc Bey had indicated that this process had 4-5 stages and had mentioned them with their coined names. If I find the possibility of reaching that sound track I would like to give

---

51 What is the place of Tefe'ul in our Religon? - https://www.sorusorcevapbul.com/soru-cevap/muhtelif/tefeul-nedir
52 Praising the Prophet (mPbuH) and His Houshold using a traditional chant.
53 Literally 'Fatiha' means 'the Opener'; it is a short surah and contains 7 versicles. It is usually recited at the beginning and end of religious activities of all sorts.
54 A Turkish pudding prepared from sesame seed and molasses or cracked wheat and pine kernels.

you that classification[55]. Oruc Bey who continues with his observations in the Sema Activity indicates that some whirlers (semazen) can perform the Sema for 9 to 10 hours. From here the subject digresses to what is possible and what is not: "Don't say 'Impossible', 'Impossible' is impossible!" According to Oruc Bey an acquaintance from the TUMATA circle who he did not mention with her name lived without eating and drinking anything for 150 days! This Lady firstly quitted eating meat and then she quitted vegetables, fruits and liquids in stages. The subject again drifts on and there is a mention of another acquaintance who was suffering from migraine. Upon his/her consultation, Oruc Bey recommended him/her the 'Diet' we mentioned earlier. According to Oruc Bey this person not only recovered from migraine pain, but also said that a taste that he/she did not have before became prevalent in his/her mouth. From quitting food the subject jumps to becoming needless, and it is mentioned that to reach the stage of becoming needless one first requires a mood of spiritual humbleness.

7TH OF JUNE 2017
(SOUND TRACK: STE039 - 114 DAY SEMA ACTIVITY- SOHBET ON THE SAME DAY FOLLOWING IFTAR - DERGAH/GOKCEDERE)

While talking about the book Fususu'l-Hikem (the Nectar of Essence) by Ibn al- Arabî , directly the subject of the Godhood of Jesus (mPbuH) opens up. While mentioning that in the past certain scholars and tribes raised the level of their Prophets to Godhood, Oruc Bey mentions the sensitivity of the subject and iterates that Allah has the power to do anything. Oruc Bey explains how to avoid making a mistake in this issue as follows: "While passing over a bridge with a car if you look at the railings you can't see the forest in the background however if you look at the forest you can't see the railings in the foreground." In other words he points to the fact that while avoiding personalization of the Prophets with God one should not overlook the Excellence of God that has emerged in the background. When Mevlana was 7 years old he wanted to see God and asked for help from his father. According to the directions of his father he began to fast for 3-5-7 days without breaking the fast and he took care to read the surah of Kevser during morning prayers. While he toiled like this for a while with the hope of seeing God, one day God All-Mighty appeared to

---

55 These happen to be 'Comparative, Regenerative and Meditative Medicine' terms.

him in the form of a human and said, "Don't exhaust yourself with these practices anymore, 'We' have raised you from the level of toil and moil to the level of witnessing."

In the sohbet which began with His Holiness Mevlana and His Holiness Shams, Oruc Bey narrates the story when His Holiness Shams threw all of the books of His Holiness Mevlana into the pond. After all of his books end up at the bottom of the pond and when Mevlana said " At least you could have spared 'that' book", His Holiness Shams put his hand into the water and gave back the aforementioned book to Mevlana in a dry and in an unspoiled state. Following events like these one passes in to areas beyond knowledge, and attention is drawn on the fact that knowledge is a very beautiful element and to reach these levels one requires intuition.

To make sure that the distinction is understood well, Oruc Bey narrates a story about Jesus (mPbuH). One day, His Holiness Jesus was seen running towards a mountain with haste, and people asked him:" Why are you running away like that?" And he said, "I am running away from the fool." And Oruc Bey goes on to define the fool as follows: "A person who pretends to know when in fact he does not."

From here the subjects jumps to 'knowing' and the fake hadiths[56]. He expresses the fact that fake hadiths were fabricated in the Emevites era. 'Ichtihad' is the activity of drawing up judgments from the sacred texts. From these one of the fake hadiths is as follows: "The ones who draw up judgments from sacred texts gains merit; the ones who draw up correct judgments gain two merits; the ones who draw up wrong judgments gain one merit." After the spreading of this hadith, the ignorant and the knowledgeable, all started drawing up judgments and degenerations were seen in the field of religion . Wrong opinions were formed. Since these types of degenerations are also present in other religions attention is drawn to the fact that every new Prophet who comes carries out a reset. Once again the sohbet returns to the hadiths and it is mentioned that there is no hadith against music. It is mentioned that some ecclesiastics pass the judgment

---

56 Hadiths are narrations of the Prophet (mPbuH), His Houshold, His geneology, His Companions, the Four Caliphs following the Prophet (mPbuH) and the 12 Imams (the Leaders -the rightfull owners of the Caliphate and Imamate) collected and carried over by Ravis (collectors and transferrers) in time.

that music is illicit, and it is immediately stated that there is no hadith about the illicitness of music. The subject drifts to the fact Islam is a rationalist religion and it is mentioned that some Benefactors give some of their advanced apprentices the permission to make their own interpretation in mystical matters.

From here the subject drifts to the concept of knowing more and the fact that humans are equal and in a vital way attention is drawn to the fact that superiority is only in impeccability (takva). The subject of being superior and at the same time being humble is brought up and Oruc Bey narrates the following story of His Holiness Mevlana: "One day when His Holiness Mevlana was passing by the Turkish Baths (Hamam) the Kulhanji (the person in charge of the fire and wood section) complained to him that he has many children but has no share in terms of worldly riches. In response His Holiness Mevlana asked him to open his mouth and soon after gold coins started pouring out of Kulhanji's mouth. All the surrounding was covered with gold. Since the gold coins were recently been cast the Kulhanji's mouth got burned from the heat. The Kulhanji thanked him a lot, and His Holiness Mevlana told him to come to him when he had difficulties with gold and silver. From the superiority in impeccability issue the subject drifts to another story related to His Holiness Mevlana: "His Holiness Mevlana entered the Turkish Baths (Hamam) one day and he immediately got out. People asked him why he got out in a rush like that. In response His Holiness Mevlana said that he saw that upon his arrival the owner of the bath sent away a person in order to open a place for him alongside the pool." Subtlety, politeness, humbleness are such graceful traits. Not to despise other people, and to follow a canonical life style... When you think and care about others the proximity with Allah increases. According to Oruc Bey, politeness, humbleness and accord among conditions should be searched.

From here the subject passes on to accord with nature and the fact that we are living among concrete buildings. The days when there was no electricity in houses are reminisced. Electricity was connected to the house of Oruc Bey's family on the day he was born. They touch upon people's pursuit of comfort and a stanza which criticizes modern brides is voiced: "What does the new bride want, a modern window, a pressure cooker, a husband without a mother and a chimney without smoke (central heating)." Following the stanza it is stated that when living within nature one does not need such formulas. One winter day a Master requested strawberries from his apprentices. All of the disciples were puzzled. Reluctantly all of them went out to search and only one disciple (who was more advanced than the others) returned with strawberries in his basket. His Master asked him how he accomplished this task; and the disciple answered that he told nature that his Master has requested strawberries and nature gave them. Oruc Bey emphasizes the fact that knowledge is very simple and unique by the following words of His Holiness Ali (mAbHF): "Knowledge was a single dot and the ignorant multiplied it." From here the subject drifts to a European tale "Jack and the Bean Stalk". Jack's adventure to another world through the means of an overgrowing bean stalk, and his encounter with the golden egg laying chicken, the slaughter of the chicken because of greed and people's loss of what they owned initially, are mentioned. The fact that over fertilizing creates barren lands is mentioned. Here Yasar Guvenc mentions life energy that should be present in the soil. Then the subject of chickens kept as prisoners in egg farms and their continuous exposure to light is brought forth. Here the important information is the fact that chicken need light in order to lay eggs. Since there is no sunlight in winter, the chicken are not able to lay eggs. From here the subject drifts to animal rights and the fact that animals are entrusted to us . And lastly Chief Judge Muhiyiddin Pervane (who lived at the time of His Holiness Mevlana) is mentioned and the sohbet ends.

6TH OF JUNE 2017

(SOUND TRACK: STE034 - 114 DAYS SEMA ACTIVITY - DERGAH/GOKCEDERE)

As I mentioned earlier sometimes questions were asked which were very general and had a very wide scope. Today's wide scope question happened to be, " What are you all doing here?". With subtle humor Oruc Bey says that repetition strengthens the nervous system and takes the story all the way from the beginning and reminds us that he studied Philosophy in the Faculty of Literature at Istanbul University. During this period he says that he was most interested in Systematic Philosophy and Logic and that he intensified his studies in Philosophical Anthropology and took some lessons in this field but he thought that this section of his study was rather short. In other words he says that he wasn't able to go into the depths of this matter. He says that anthropology is the science of humans and encompasses all other sections of science. He says that the graduation thesis that he presented here had the title: "Mankind in Mevlana". He narrates that around about that time he got acquainted with two Mevlevite Sheikhs and in 1980 his connections with Europe began. Here he mentions that around 18 or 19 years ago during a seminar on His Holiness Mevlana in Switzerland, the sema idea that we are now undertaking came into view. The subject drifts to the book The Legends of the Enlightened Ones by Ahmed Eflâkî. Oruc Bey says that this work was formed by Eflâkî via the expansion of the book called Risale-i Sipehsalar written by the author Sipehsalar, by adding his own knowledge about the events at the time of His Holiness Mevlana. From this book we learn that His Holiness Mevlana performed many times 3 days and nights, 3 times 7 days and nights, once 9 days and nights, once 16 days and nights and 3 times 40 nights and nights sema. According to the narrations His Holiness Mevlana completed these semas sometimes uninterruptedly and sometimes by giving prayer and sohbet breaks. It is narrated that His Holiness had 3 groups of musicians ready and they performed in a rotating fashion and they were wretched during the long sema events.

The traditional semas performed today on the other hand are 35-45 minutes long and due to the recital of the Eulogy of Mevlana and the Holy Qoran the sema section lasts for just around 30 minutes. Oruc Bey who explains that this type of sema tradition is based on a vision seen by Adil Chelebi while he was in a state of trance and the old type of sema continued in the Afion Mevlevihane and he continues his talk by saying that here even Lady Sheikhs were present.

He says that he carries written ratification (ijazet) from the Mevlevi Sheikh Turgut Baba, the Bahariye Mevlevihane Dede Ali Fani Dede and Ziyâ Dede and notes that they initially performed the first 3 days and nights sema in Switzerland. Following Switzerland, sema activities were continued in Turkey, Germany and Spain. Oruc Bey who says that until today 31 times 3 days and nights, 5 times 5 days and nights, 7 times 7 days and nights, once 9 days and nights, once 16 days and nights, 3 times 40 days and nights, once 66 days and nights and once 99 days and nights semas were carried out and now they are within the 114 days and nights sema activity which corresponds to the number of surahs in the Holy Qoran.

They continue the talk with the fact that changes don't distort the essence and the Bible was modified with the Council in Nicosia (Iznik/Turkey). They mention the strife between Pavlos and Barnabas. They address

the fact that a Mevlevite Sheikh once said that there is not much differ-
ence between the Christianity of Jesus (mPbuH) and Islam. Oruc Bey
who iterates that essentially their main area of focus is sema, indicates
that they were not able explain what they are doing here to other people,
including journalists and even professors.

Oruc Bey who indicates that these type of organizations can all be carried out with unity also mentions that the Dergah was visited by people
from Mauritius, Fiji and Martinique. Oruc Bey expresses that while they
were organizing these sema activities with his spouse they had concerns
about the budget but thanking God he says that they did not have any
problems about this issue until now. Oruc Bey who indicates that during
the sema activity one day over 500 people were hosted but despite the
number no one was left without food, the kitchen worked in an extra-or-
dinary fashion and these were only possible with feelings of trust, belief,
dedication, fraternity and sense of sharing.

Oruc Bey says that Turgut Baba once told him that the first ayets of the
surah of Bakara define the sema; and the ayets (versicles) are as follows:

> "Those who abstain and who believe in the unmanifest and are upon
> correct prayer ; we giveth them their livelihood and they spend from
> that for the sake of Allah; they believe what is revealed to you and to
> what is revealed to the ones before you."[57]

Oruc Bey who touches on the moment when Allah proclaimed, "
Am I not your Lord?" and draws attention to the words of Mevlana
where he says, "Sema is the moment when you hear that proclama-
tion and say 'Yes!'"

Oruc Guvenc who mentions that sema infused belief to many non-be-
lievers and became a remedy to their problems addresses the question
"Why are we doing the sema?" as follows:

> "Some forms of worship are with time. The 'Teravih Prayer'[58] which is
> the longest namaz takes around an hour. However , we have friends
> who continue to whirl up to 9-10 hours. From here the door is
> opened to permanent namaz!

---

57 Surah of Bakara 3rd and 4th versicles: They believe in the unmanisfest, they perform namaz, and
spend for the sake of Allah from what we giveth to them. They believe what was revealed to you
and what was revealed to the ones before you. They have also belived truly in the afterlife.
58 The 33 reqat prayer following the breaking of the fast during the month of Ramadan.

Is doing long semas a feat? Yes! ... The trick is to lift the doubts and the veils in our minds. Before getting into action, the information of that action permeates to the self of that person. Mature people prevent negative thoughts when they arise and create a second body which is produced through will!"

Here a page from the "The Legends of the Enlightened Ones" is opened (pages 182-183, 98th and the 99th narration).

Shemseddin Muallim never performed the sema but stood in front of Mevlana while he was whirling and watched his face. "One day when His Holiness Mevlana asked him about this, Shemseddin Muallim answered him as follows: "I can't think of anything that is nicer and more acceptable than watching your face." In response His Holiness Mevlana replied: "We also have an unseen face. Try to see it from now on so that when we leave you can immediately recognize it and see it." After this conversation Shemseddin Muallim begins doing the Sema.

It is mentioned that sema is not a form entertainment and the following conclusion is voiced: "Sema is a form of worship!"

99. Narration

Bahaddin Bahrî known as 'the Clerk of Secrets' narrates the following: "One day I asked His Holiness Mevlana "What is the illness of the Sheikhs?". His Holiness Mevlana replied as follows: "Real Sheikhs don't have any illnesses, only the ones who have been dismissed from the Dergah (due to arrogance or impertinence) may catch these illnesses." In those times there was a Sheikh called Sheikh Nasreddin and he was neck and neck in terms of knowledge with Sheikh Sadreddin. One day while His Holiness Mevlana and his students were passing by the sohbet abode of this person and his disciples, Sheikh Nasreddin made some overdone and arrogant remarks about the path and the genealogy of His Holiness Mevlana. And he added that he didn't think that His Holiness Mevlana had any radiance. His Holiness Mevlana who somehow heard these comments made some harsh remarks indicating that he was speaking in an incorrect way and Sheikh Nasreddin fell to ground with a grunt. His disciples swarmed around him; Sheikh Nasreddin recovered his consciousness slightly and confessed that he made some wrong remarks. And said that his words reached His Holiness Mevlana from an unmanifest path and that he had received a celestial blow. At that moment our Prophet (mPbuH) was resting in a lying down position but his heart was open to issues related to mankind. When he realized what was taking place Sheikh Nasreddin lost his power. The disciples of His Holiness Mevlana checked the surroundings but they could not find the subject of his harsh remarks. With tears in their eyes they asked him about the person who was the subject of his remarks. His Holiness Mevlana proclaimed, "Faithless Nasreddin lost his power." "In his diabolical abode he was making evil comments about us and thereupon he lost his power. The All-Mighty God made an example of him for the world."

Oruc Bey who says that one can derive lessons from this story repeats the following words of His Holiness Mevlana; "Nothing remains hidden, and presumptions don't benefit anyone" and adds, "You talk about carry-over information in front of the Qutb of the Time[59] and your soul which finds peace through divine revelation scolds you!" Oruc Bey mentions that blabbing about the Mystics may cause serious difficult situations in life. From here they pass onto technical and daily subjects and the sohbet ends.

5TH OF JUNE 2017
(SOUND TRACK: STE028 - 114 DAYS SEMA ACTIVITY - DERGAH/GOKCEDERE)
As always Oruc Bey's asks me to bring his attaché case and instructs me on how to close it properly. He admonishes me to exert some effort until I hear a 'click' or a snapping sound. He iterates that he has been using this case for years. Oruc Bey says that he will not be available in the Dergah for a few days and he informs people that they have been invited to a congress.

He says that the activities carried out in the Dergah have a historical mission and hereupon the subject drifts to His Holiness Mevlana. According to the explanations of Oruc Bey the written work on His Holiness Mevlana and his family had been put into word while His Holiness Mevlana was still alive. Following his death the stories about his children were also recorded. Oruc Bey says the following: "We believe in these

---

59 Qutb of the Time is the person who is to most knowledgeable person of the time and is appointed on earth by the rule of the heavens for a certain period in Time.

narrations and they have not been refuted or modified. As you know there are feats and miraculous events in the life of His Holiness Mevlana." The subject drifts to the miracles of the Prophets. He explains that since the Prophets are on the path of Allah, through the beneficence of Allah such events emerge. As an example he gives the talking of Jesus (mPbuH) when he was only a baby. From here the subject comes to our Prophet (mPbuH).

Our Prophet (mPbuH) took part in many long journeys with his Grandfather and his Uncle. One day when they were traveling in Syria a (Christian) Priest called Bahira was watching them. He came to the caravan and said that he wanted to host them. When his uncle asked Prophet Muhammed to stay behind to watch the caravan Bahira was a bit saddened because it was the Prophet Muhammed (mPbuH) that he intended to invite in the first place. The Priest Bahira wanted to look between the shoulder blades of Prophet Muhammed and there he saw a sign. This is called the 'Seal of Prophecy'. And the Priest Bahira said that this Individual is the Prophet of the Time. The caravan was going towards Yemen but Bahira learned that those areas were bit dangerous at that time and informed them about it. When he was asked why you wanted to host the Prophet (mPbuH), the Priest said that there is a cloud which follows him , wherever he goes the cloud goes with him, when he stops the cloud also stops and this is written in our book. Also written in book is the seal that our Prophet (mPbuH) carries on his body.

Oruc Bey continues and asks, "What kind of a book did this Priest read and why don't other priests know this book?" Secondarily he says that Prophets have some special marks on them and Allah All-Mighty creates some extraordinary events around them and makes these a reason for the guidance of people.

Hereupon the subject drifts back to His Holiness Mevlana. It is mentioned that his father Sultanu'l-Ulema Bahaddin Veled was a great leader possessing a very wide scoped spiritual background. While being reminded that jealous people exists in every era of human history it is stated that His Holiness Bahaddin Veled was informed against to the Sultan of that time using a slander. The content of the slander was as follows: It was informed to the Sultan that Bahaddin Veled was trying to claim the Sultanate. Hereupon His Holiness Bahaddin Veled decided to make a journey to Anatolia. The mufti[60] who were the perpetrators of the slander - they were

60 Muslim clerics who had the authority to issue religious decrees (fetva) and who were responsible
  for the religious affairs in provinces and counties

are around 300 people in total - saw the same dream that night. Upon this event they all came to apologize and said that they could not properly understand him. Oruc Bey who indicates that dreams come into play when verbal explanations don't achieve any results iterates that despite the apology, His Holiness Bahaddin Veled and his cortège made a 7 year journey and arrived in Anatolia and during this trip His Holiness Mevlana found the opportunity to meet many Great Sufis. The Seljukian Sultan of the time showed great respect to His Holiness Bahaddin Veled and he allocated a 'Medrese' (a university) for him so that he could continue his activities. Following the passing away of his father His Holiness Mevlana continued the lessons there. His expositions found abhorrent reflections in people with dogmatic mentatlity and at around these times feats and small miracles became manifest in His Holiness Mevlana. Dogmatics, people who accused him, people who tried to race with him all swarmed around him and due to these events, permeation of his of his thoughts and their acceptance became easier. Since then 800 years have passed but when we open a page from the Masnavi the subjects that come up are subjects that today's science is investigating.

Following these explanations of Oruc Bey a "tefe'ul" is made from the book Menakibu'l-Arifiin (the Stories of the Enlightened Ones) and a person who came from India to visit the Dergah is asked to open a page. I had talked with this youngster previously and had learned that he was the disciple of a Hindu Master. In my YouTube channel you can find his notably long Hindu Chant which he implemented in the Dergah. The place he opened happened to be the 225th page and the 174th story. A Hindu Raja sends a letter to Sheikh Sadi-i Shirazi. Here Oruc Bey draws attention to the fact that the subject is related to a Hindu Ruler. The Hindu Ruler asks His Holiness Sadi to send him the ode (gazel) that he most likes. Thereupon His Holiness Shirazi sends a new ode that just arrived from His Holiness Mevlana.

The ode (gazel) is as follows:

Every moment, from the right and the left sounds of love are presenting themselves.
And we are heading there so that we can look on.
Who wants to take part in this spectacle?

His Holiness Shirazi adds the following note to his letter:

"In Anatolia a Holy Sultan has emerged, and this is a section of his work. There is no word more beautiful than this, and nothing more beautiful will ever be pronounced. To visit this Sultan I want to travel to Anatolia. I want to prostrate myself and plead before him. Let our Sultan be informed of the situation thuswise."

When the Ruler Shemseddin-i Hindi read this he shed tears. He ordered a great come together and they whirled to the tune of that ode (gazel). This ruler also sent many gifts to Sheikh Sadi to express his gratitude. Here Oruc Bey draws attention to the fact that although His Holiness Mevlana is located in Konia they are doing the sema (whirling) in Shiraz. In the sequel of the story Sheikh Sadi-i Shirazi comes to Konia and kisses the hand of His Holiness Mevlana and receives the blessing of the dervishes.

The Ruler Shemseddin-i Hindi used to follow the path of Master Seyfeddin Baharzi. He put this ode on paper and sent it to His Holiness Seyfeddin Baharzi together with other gifts. At that time all the scholars of Bokhara were around this Sheikh. Here Oruc Bey draws attention to the fact that the event is taking place in Bokhara. When the Sheikh read the ode (gazel) he screamed and fainted. He became very excited, he tore off his clothes, screamed and said the following:

"What a coy valiant man,
What a cavalier of religion,
What a Qutb of the sky and earth,

Indeed a strange Sultan has emerged in this world. The people who are open to revelation were yearning for such a personage. They tried to attain their goal through the beneficence of Allah but it wasn't destined to be. This feat was granted to the posteriors.

Poem:

"The Fortune that the passing centuries searched for in their dreams,
Was granted to the people living in recent times..."

The story had started at a page before the place which the Hindu youngster had opened; Oruc Bey says that now they have reached that page and continues the story.

"... Oh Lord! We should search for that personage with an iron rawhide sandal and an iron wand. Here is our will to our friends: Whoever has the power to walk, whoever possesses the strength should visit that King; thuswise he will attain bounty and blessings from the ancestors of His Holiness Bahaddin Veled who were great Sheikhs. Their ninth ancestor is His Holiness Ebu Bekir[61] (The Most Righteous)"

Here Oruc Bey Draws attention to the fact that the father of His Holiness Mevlana comes from the genealogy of His Holiness Ebu Bekir.

"... May Allah bless them all. I am very weak and have grown old. I cannot withstand the tribulations of travel. If I had the power I would go there walking not on my foot but on my head."

The grandson of Sheikh Muzhiruddin was also at that gathering.

"Oh Muzhiruddin, I am hopeful that your face will be illuminated with the luminance of that holy personage. Through the will of Allah don't fail to communicate our respects to him."

Following the death of his father, Sheikh Muzhiruddin set out for Anatolia. And he became blissed by visiting that holy personage. He extended the Greetings and the longing of his father to His Holiness Mevlana. And His Holiness Mevlana placated him. Muzhiruddin stayed in Konia for a few years and then returned to Bokhara. It is said that one of his sons is buried in Konia.

At this moment since they are related Oruc Bey enters on the 175th story.

When the news of this gazel and the emergence of His Holiness Mevlana spreads all over kingdoms the Sheikhs of Bokhara and Dest flood into Anatolia and by visiting His Holiness Mevlana they try to discover new realms in the abstract. It is said that 20 people from Samarkand and Bokhara came and settled in Konia and became his disciples.

Here Oruc Bey ends the story and brings the subject to feats, accordingly with what was mentioned above. Oruc Bey indicates that feats can be composed of a word, a letter or even a scratch and begins to narrate another story. In the Ottoman times there was famous calligrapher. He was going to cross the Bosphorus from the European side to the Asian side. In those days there were no undersea tunnels, ferries and similar ameni-

---

61 His Holiness Ebu Bekir (ra) is one of the Companions of Our Prophet (mPbuH) and is is the first Calipha succeeding Him. Also he was the person who took refugee in a cave with the Prophet (mPbuH) when polytheists were chasing them in order to kill them. His title 'Syddyk' means 'the most righteous'.

ties; if you wanted the cross the Bosphorus you had to get on a boat. The calligrapher got on a boat but realized that he had no money on him. In those days the calligraphers carried their pen and paper on them. He drew an 'Elif' (Alpha) on a piece of paper and told the boatman that he did not have any money on him but he could get quite a bit of money for this piece of paper if he showed it at the used-book bazaar in Bajezid (a neighborhood on the European side of the Bosphorus). The boatman did not believe him but did not say anything and let him a free ride. He took the paper and put it in his pocket. Weeks followed, one day the boatman was passing by the used-book bazaar and he had the paper with him. He was curious about whether it would fetch any money. He showed the paper to a second-hand book seller and told him its story. Immediately a commotion began in all the shops around and he heard voices saying things like this piece must belong to calligrapher so and so...etc. All shop owners bid to buy this piece of calligraphy. In the end it was sold for a big sum. The boatman was very pleased. Again weeks followed. The calligrapher once again coincided with the same boatman; the boatman recognized him immediately but the famous calligrapher did not remember him. They started crossing the Bosphorus. The calligrapher made a move to present him the fare but the boatman rejected it and asked him to make another 'elif' (the letter Alpha in the Arabic alphabet) on a paper! Oruc Bey says that we should not dismiss even an 'Elif' and iterates that the legacy of Mystics and the Friends of Allah guide people from generation to generation.

Here they open a page from the Masnavi and continue. They ask a European artist present in the audience to open a page. Oruc Bey indicates that this lady takes part in the Semas very often and tells of all her merits and notes that she is giving lessons at the Waldorf Steiner School of Art. She chooses the 5th volume and opens the pages 208-209. The number of the story is 2537. The beginning of the subject is at page 206. A man takes refuge in a house. He has gone pale. The landlord asks what is the matter with him. The man replies as follows:

"They are catching all of the donkeys in the streets to entertain the Cruel King." The landlord says: "Is that true! But you are not a donkey. Why the worry?" The man replies as follows: "The men are set to work in such a rage that if they catch me thinking me as a donkey I wouldn't be surprised. If people without the ability to distinguish seize power they may take the owner of the donkey thinking him as a donkey also."

"Fear not our King won't take action out of place. He has the ability of distinction. He hears everything and sees everything. Change your way and don't fear the donkey catchers. Of the Jesus of our time, fear not you are not a donkey. The fourth level of the heavens is full of your luminance. Perish the thought! Your port of call is not a barn. You are in the barn because of a mission but you excel the stars in the sky. A master and a donkey are different things. Not everyone who enters a barn is a donkey. Why are we following the tracks of donkeys? Tell me about roses and rose gardens. Tell me about the pomegranate, the orange apple branch, wine and countless beauties; or tell me about the waves made of pearls, tell me of birds who gather roses and lay silver or golden eggs; tell me of birds who feed gazelles and who fly on their backs and also fly facedown. In the universe there are secret staircases that lead to the heavens step by step; each cloud has a separate staircase; and every gait has a different sky. And each one of them is oblivious of the other; it is an extensive country, with no beginning or end. One of them is baffled and says how cute, and the other is astonished and says why is he so baffled (they are amazed of each other). The earth is wide, there trees sprout from the ground, and grow tall. The leaves on the trees are shocked and say what a beautiful and wide country! The nightingales tweet and fly in curls around gazelles asking them to give something from what they eat. (Now Oruc Bey says that they have reached the opened page.) There is no end to these words. You should once again return to the story of the fox, the lion, that disease and hunger...Oruc Bey intervenes here and tells the beginning of the story of the lion, the fox and the donkey. "At the beginning of the story the lion is hungry but is very old. He offers bribes to the fox. And the fox tries to bring the donkey to the lion through mischievous means. Let's see how we will benefit from this story."

The fox took the donkey to the meadow. The lion wanted to attack the donkey and tear it into pieces. The lion was a little bit far from the donkey. When he saw the donkey he lost his patience because of his greed and did not wait until the donkey came closer. He suddenly roared fearsomely. But he had no power to move. When the donkey saw this he galloped away until he reached the mountain foot. The fox said: " Oh my King; why did you lose your patience during the struggle? If you had let him come closer you would have overpowered him. HASTE IS THE TRICKERY OF THE DEVIL. (Oruc Bey indicates that we have reached the point of spiritual nourishment.) PATIENCE AND PRECAUTION IS THE BLESSING OF GOD. He was far away and saw your move and ran away. He noticed your weakness."

The lion said, "I thought I had all the buttons. I did not think I was so feeble. But hunger and need exceeded my patience. Because of hunger I lost my patience and my mind... If you can, trick him again and bring him here one more time. Be deceptive and try to bring him here. I will be grateful." The fox said, "Alright." "If God is willing I will mesmerize him with blindness. If he forgets his blindness that's a fine kettle of fish! And this is very probable because of he is an ass. However, if I fool him and bring him here don't show haste again."

"Yes, I checked myself and I don't have my luster anymore, I am feeling very weak. I won't move until the donkey comes very close. I'll pretend to be asleep."

The fox set off. He was grumbling on his way:

"Oh My Lord! Help me so that the donkey behaves in an unwary way. I know that the donkey had repented to God many times not to be fooled. Let me ruin his prayers and his repentance. We are the enemies of the mind and promises."

What significance does the mind -made of the revolutions of the planet Saturn (Zuhal)- have over the total mind of the universes (akl-i kull)? That mind receives blessing in Mercury (Utarit) and Mars (Zuhal) -this time Oruc Bey interprets Zuhal as Mars. And we receive beneficence and knowledge from the God whose attributes are blessing and benefaction. Our goal is the knowledge present in the level of Allah. Here Oruc Bey reminds us that this type of knowledge is known as 'Ilm-i Ledûn ' in Sufism. That sun made of moons has disciplined us. That is why we keep saying Allah is All-Mighty.

The fox says the following: "Although the donkey is aware of my trickery with this deception he will forget all about it. Maybe he will be in a donkey mood and will forget his repentance and be fooled. BREAKING A PROMISE AND FORGETTING YOUR REPENTANCE WILL GET YOU CURSED. The Jews who were admonished about the Saturday prohibition broke their promise and they were mutated. The God turned them into apes. Why?...Because they were obstinate and broke their vow with God. This religious community will not be mutated, but Oh the Wise Man, their hearts and souls will be mutated. If the heart of a man turns into the heart of an ape his body will be ranked even lower than an ape. If the donkey had any merit he wouldn't fall into such a situation in the first place. However the dog of the Seven Sleepers was good natured."

Here Oruc Bey digresses to the event of the Seven Sleepers described in the Surah of Kehf in the Holy Qoran. "They slept in a cave for 360 years. And they had a dog with them. He had the form of a dog. Did this form diminish anything from his excellence? The Jews were mutated so that the people were able to see the wrath of God visually. They were transformed into pigs and donkeys because they broke their vow."

Now they return to the fox again. It is said that the fox devised something and came immediately to the side of the donkey.

Donkey: "I should be aware of friends like you. Oh cruel creature, what did I do to you so that you took me to the dragon? Why did you hold a grudge against me? Was there any other reason besides the evil in your creation?" As you know, the scorpion stung the foot of a youngster but the youngster had not done anything bad to the scorpion. Just like the Devil; our leathal enemy, although we have done nothing against him. The Devil is an enemy of people because of his nature. He enjoys the destruction of humans. He is continuously messing around. The evil inside him calls him to animosity without any reason. Every moment he calls you to a Pavilion in order to throw you down a well. He tries to throw you to the pool head first. That cursed creature even fooled Adam whose heart was open to divine revelation and who had his eyes open. Adam had no sin in the past. He never injured him or did anything to him that was unjust.

The fox said: "That was a spell; he appeared as a lion to your eyes. As your companion I am weaker than you are corporally. Despite this I graze there day and night. There are dragons and monsters in this world; if there was no spell would everything be still green? I was going to tell you not to be afraid if you see anything, but since I was feeling sorry for you it slipped my mind. When I saw you running away I called you to my side. I was going to tell you of the spell; I was going to say that you are seeing an illusion but there is no truth in it."

Here Oruc Bey says that the story is very long and continues for a long time and stops the narration. He says that in the story there are intriguing points: "One of them is to make a vow (promise) and to keep it. And the cunning of the fox... There is a verse in the Qoran, which says: "The Devil can see you from a point where you can't see him." That is why we have to be very careful, keep our vows and promises, and make good on them."

Here Oruc Bey ends his talk by giving some important directives about manners and behavior in the Dergah. I don't want to leave out the end of the story. The fox uses his cunning and takes the donkey to the lion once again. The lion tears the donkey apart and eats a portion of the donkey then while he leaves to drink some water the fox comes and eats the heart and the liver of the donkey. When the lion returns he asks where the heart and the liver of the donkey have gone to. The fox again uses his cunning and says that folk who are like donkeys don't have a heart or a liver. In fables like these the aim is to give lessons by making animals talk like humans.

I have many recordings of Oruc Bey's sohbets; however, my aim is not to present them in a transcribed manner. My main aim is to acquaint you with the atmosphere of the sohbets and share with the reader a few memoirs by adding them where appropriate.

I would like to end my book by presenting some information under the title "Hodja Ahmet Yesevî and Turkhood" in the next chapter.

HODJA AHMED YESEVÎ AND TURKHOOD

I had previously informed you that the ethnic origins of Oruc Bey reach out to Central Asia. Following the independence of former Turkic Soviet Republics, and the emergence of their musical heritage alongside with their other cultural extravagances had shown the world the presence of a wide-ranged Turkic musical culture. Oruc Bey had begun to compile, evaluate and present this cultural heritage which he was aware of since his childhood and which he had the chance to closely examine during their Soviet Union trip, long before the dissolution of the Soviet Union and apart from using them in musical performances he had also started to use these tunes in music therapy sessions. This cultural presence was not just a musical heritage. Elements of history, heroes, wars, founded states, weapons of the era, items of Sufism, foods and dishes, costumes and many other factors etc. were fragments of this cultural heritage.

Another figure Oruc Bey put great emphasis on was His Holiness Hodja Ahmed Yesevî (known as Hazreti Turkestan)[62]. He had reserved a special place to this Holy Mystic which was one of the great monuments of Turkhood and he had always mentioned him and his disciple Hadji Bektash-i Velî by attaching a particular importance on them. Here I would like to share some of what was narrated about them in the sohbets.

During an expedition (holy battle) people resorted to our Prophet (mPbuH) for food. But there was no food available anywhere. Hereupon Our Prophet (mPbuH) prayed to Allah and Angel Gabriel (mPbuH) descended from the heavens with a tray full of dates. During the distribution of the dates one date fell to the ground. And Angel Gabriel (mPbuH) said that this date belongs to Ahmed who will come 400 years later. Our Prophet (mPbuH) asked who would like to take this date to him. And Arslan Baba stepped forward. Our Prophet (mPbuH) placed the date onto the palate of Arslan Baba and Arslan Baba met Hodja Ahmed Yesevî (Ahmed) 400 years later on a bridge in the township of Seyran (Sayram) in Turkestan. Hodja Ahmet Yesevî was 6 or 7 at that time. They both recognized each other. Hodja Ahmed Yesevî asked, "Where is my date?" and Arslan Baba presented him the date and was involved with the guidance of Hodja Ahmet Yesevî for a few years. It is said that the Caliphate was passed onto the

---

62 Literally this means 'His Holiness Turkestan'

Turks all the way back then with that date.[63]

When the Mystics in Turkestan gathered, since Hodja Ahmet Yesevî was only 10-12 at that time they were hesitant to accept him among them because he hadn't come of age. While they were discussing this issue they concluded that if Hodja Ahmet Yesevî laid the table in their house belonging to his father they will accept that he had come of age. Without any difficulty Hodja Ahmet Yesevî laid the table and was accepted among the mystics of Turkestan. Of course in this story symbols and the particular meanings belonging to the world of abstract come into question.

NARRATION

One day, when he came for a sohbet Hyzyr (mPbuH)[64] found Hodja Ahmet Yesevî troubled and sad when in fact he usually saw him jovial and content. And with astonishment asked the reason for his state of mood: "It is a fact that every day I circle around the world seven times to find a comrade, someone I can talk to and since I can't find anyone better than you I always seek your company. Since I know that you have attained exalted and sublime levels I am wondering why you are in such a sad state? Why is this sorrow?"

And Hodja Ahmed Yesevî replied to Hyzyr (mPbuH) as follows:

"For days my disciples have acquired a mood of distress, and gloom has appeared in their hearts which has ruined their peace. The mental mood of our friends and our brothers has been flooded with worries; since I find no way to eliminate this I am left with a sad and troubled mood. This is my definite duty as their Master. However, I wasn't able to remove the mood of distress over them. This is why I feel sad; this is the reason for my sorrow."

When Hyzyr (mPbuH) received this response from Hodja Ahmed Yesevî, he immediately began the zikr (chant) by saying, "Allah" and described the zikr-i erre (the rip saw chant) to His Holiness Sultan Yesevi and recommended that he instruct his disciples to carry out this chant as well. Hereupon when His Holiness Ahmed Yesevî and His Holiness Hyzyr (mPbuH) instructed the disciples to do the rip

---

63 Source: Yasar Guvenc

64 The Green Prophet (mPbuH) mentioned in detail in the surah of Kehf in the Holy Qoran. He is known to posses special knowledge from the level of Allah. He never dies and lives eternally. One section of this surah was used as a theme in the film 'the Silent Flute' starring David Carradine.

saw chant; the mood of gloom dissipated and the acolytes' hearts achieved a mood of relief. Following the disappearance of the mood of gloom, this rip saw zikr (chant) became a regular practice among the disciples of His Holiness Turkestan and became a regular prayer and a ritual for the Yesevite lineage.

With this narration we learn how the ripsaw zikr (zikr-i erre) came to be a part of the Yesevite practices and its base and its essence. This is the reason why the Yesevite Order is considered to be among the Jehriyye[65].

Sultan Ahmed Hazînî who recorded and noted this narration from Cevâhiru'l-Ebrâr, states that from that day on His Holiness Ahmed Yesevî instructed his disciples to do the rip saw chant and that this chant was continued after his death and that many Mystics who reached his time performed this chant and made wishes for it to continue until doomsday.[66]

I have heard different versions of this story many times from Oruc Bey. The rip saw chant is performed by bending forward while exhaling and saying "Al..." and straightening up and inhaling while saying "lah!" and continuing this routine; and it is a very relieving and relaxing zikr. Since I personally performed this zikr in the past, I think it was appropriate for me to say a few words to explain things further.

It is said that Hodja Ahmed Yesevî had over 300,000 disciples. And one of them was Hadji Bektash-i Velî. One day, a female mystic known as Kadinjik Ana threw a piece of burning wood with the power of guardianship. This ember fell to Anatolia. Hadji Bektash-i Velî was asked to find this piece of ember and build a Dergah at the place where it was found and start his mission of guidance. And hereupon Hodja Ahmed Yesevî sent Hadji Bektash-i Velî to Anatolia disguised as a pigeon.

When the Anatolian Mystics gathered they felt something like a burdensomeness leaning on them and agreed that there was something wrong and decided to send Karacaahmet Sultan to investigate disguised as a sparrowhawk. Following a research Karacaahmet Sultan determined the fact that all pigeons were flying in couples but one pigeon was flying single and made a report to the delegation. The delegation demanded the apprehension of the pigeon and just when Karacaahmet Sultan disguised as

---

65 'Jehriyye' refers to groups who chant (perform zikr) loudly in contrats to silent chant which is refered to as 'Hafiyye'.

66 Pîr-i Turkistan Hoca Ahmed Yesevî (In memorial of the UNESCO 2016 Hodja Ahmed Yesevî year),Dr. Hayati Bice, Ankara, 2016

a sparrowhawk was about to catch the single pigeon the pigeon suddenly transformed into a human and caught the sparrowhawk. When the two mystic transformed into their normal human form and started talking with each other Hadji Bektash-i Velî asked, " Do you remember the hand that gave you a grant in the recent gathering of foreordination?" Karacaahmet Sultan said, " Yes, it had a green mole on it." Hadji Bektash-i Velî opened his hand and Karacaahmet Sultan observed the green mole. Karacaahmet Sultan hereupon re-transformed into a sparrowhawk and set off for the Anatolian Mystics.

There are many versions of the story and they have all morphed into a mythology among Anatolian people. Up to here, the narration has been taken from Yasar Guvenc; the elder brother of Oruc Bey. Following this incident Anatolian Mystics led by Seyyid Mahmud Hayranî who happened to be riding a lion and was holding a snake in his hand as a whip arrived in Sulukaracahoyuk where Hadji Bektash-i Velî lived. When Hadji Bektash-i Velî saw this he mounted a wall and leapt forward and said, "the real feat is to make something that is inanimate to advance." When Anatolian Mystics saw this they accepted the sublime emanations that have emerged in Hadji Bektash-i Velî.

The mausoleum of His Holiness Hodja Ahmed Yesevî, im Kazakhstan. The image is a reconstruction using effects.

It is said that the piece of wood that Kadinjik Ana threw with the hand of guardianship belonged to a hackberry tree and that leafed tree still exists in Sulukaracahoyuk.

One day Sheikh Lokman Perende (the Caliph of Hodja Ahmed Yesevî) went on a pilgrimage to Hajj. While they rested for prayer (vakfe) on Mount Arafat, Pishi (a Turkic confectionary like shortbread) came to his mind. And he said to people who were with him: "This is the eve of a festivity, where I live it is tradition to prepare Pishi and hand them out to others." When Hadji Bektash-i Velî was informed of this through the abstract (telepathically) he immediately snatched a tray of Pishi cooked by the local ladies and by the knowledge belonging to the level of Allah (ilm-i ledûn) he folded space (tayy-i mekan) and in an instant went to the Kaaba and fulfilled the wish of his Sheikh. His Sheikh made many compliments to him and honored him by saying, "This person is a true pilgrim (Hadji)." The first section of the name Hadji Bektash-i Velî is based on this incident.

Previously, I had mentioned that the TUMATA Group had won 3rd place prize in a song contest in Neftkamsk (Bashkurtistan). Three years later, during a trip to Kyrgyzstan following an invitation, everyone on the trip decided to go to the city of Turkistan in Kazakhstan. After travelling eight or nine hours, they arrived just in time for the morning prayer and on a Kandil[67] day they reached the place where the mausoleum of His Holiness Hodja Ahmed Yesevî was located. According to what we heard, at that time the government of Kazakhstan was restoring the mausoleum and the ceramics through a Turkish firm.[68]

---

67 Religious days when certain moments of importance of Islam are observed as a religious festivity.
68 Source: Yasar Guvenc

From the Left to the Right: Kanikey Guvenc-Akcay (His daughter), Oruc Bey, Suyumbike Guvenc-Noris (his daughter) and Andrea Azize Guvenc (his wife)

EPILOGUE

Oruc Bey passed away (physically, at least) as a result of a heart attack following surgery on the 5th of July 2017. He still lives among us through his spiritual entity.

ASST. PROF. DR.
RAHMI ORUC GUVENC
1948 - ∞